BOLT

ULTIMATE SPORTS HEROES

John Murray has written and edited books on a wide range of sports, from athletics and Australian rules football to tennis and Test cricket. He is the sports director at *Touchline*.

Cover illustration by Dan Leydon.
To learn more about Dan visit danleydon.com
To purchase his artwork visit etsy.com/shop/footynews
Or just follow him on Twitter @danleydon

BOLT

JOHN MURRAY

DINO

Published by Dino Books
an imprint of John Blake Publishing,
3 Bramber Court, 2 Bramber Road,
London W14 9PB, England

www.johnblakebooks.com

www.facebook.com/johnblakebooks ◼
twitter.com/jblakebooks ◼

This edition published in 2017

ISBN: 978 1 78606 467 7

British Library Cataloguing-in-Publication Data:

A catalogue record for this book is available from the British Library.

Design by www.envydesign.co.uk

Printed and bound in Great Britain by Clays Ltd, St Ives plc

3 5 7 9 10 8 6 4 2

Papers used by John Blake Publishing are natural, recyclable products made from
wood grown in sustainable forests. The manufacturing processes conform to the
environmental regulations of the country of origin.

Every attempt has been made to contact the relevant copyright-holders, but some
were unobtainable. We would be grateful if the appropriate people could contact us.

John Blake Publishing is an imprint of Bonnier Publishing
www.bonnierpublishing.co.uk

For Clare and Beth

TABLE OF CONTENTS

CHAPTER 1

THE GREATEST

Usain Bolt stood on the track and waited. He had just 100 metres left to run in his Olympic career. After three Olympic Games and a sackful of medals and memorable moments, it had all come down to this final moment.

He looked around the magnificent Olympic Stadium in Rio de Janeiro. Sixty thousand fans were packed into the venue, ready to watch the final of the 4x100m relay. Many of them were cheering his name.

'We love you, Usain.'

'Let's make it three out of three, Usain.'

'I want to see the Lightning Bolt!'

He had first burst onto the international scene at

the Beijing Olympics eight years earlier, stunning the world when he recorded the fastest ever times in the 100m, 200m and relay. Then, four years later, he was the superstar of the London Games, sprinting to another three gold medals.

Now in Rio, with the 100m and 200m golds already safely packed away in his suitcase, Usain had the chance to record an historic treble. In the relay, he wanted to give the fans one last spectacular performance to remember.

He took a deep breath. He had been here so many times before, in so many high-pressure races, but he couldn't help but feel a little nervous. Unlike the individual events where he could control his own destiny, he relied on his teammates in the relay. Each team was made up of four athletes, and Usain would need his fellow Jamaicans to be on top form if they were to win gold. Luckily, in Asafa Powell, Yohan Blake and Nickel Ashmeade, he knew his country had some of the fastest men on the planet.

It was nearly time. In less than forty seconds, his Olympic career would be over.

'Come on, boys. Just get the baton safely round to me – then I'll do the rest,' said Usain, who would run the last leg of the relay.

No one could hear a word he said, though. It was too loud because of all the fans' screaming.

At last the crowd fell silent as they waited for the starter's gun.

Bang!

The crowd roared. They were off.

Asafa burst out of the blocks. Usain was standing on the far side of the track, but he could see that his teammate was running a great first leg. Jamaica were neck-and-neck with the USA as Asafa handed the baton to Yohan Blake.

Immediately to Yohan's left was the American Justin Gatlin, Usain's great rival. They had enjoyed some terrific battles over the years, but Usain had always held the upper hand – and he was desperate to keep it that way tonight.

'Come on, Yohan' he said. 'Run like the wind.'

There was still nothing to choose between the two teams as Nickel took the baton for the third leg. Usain got into position. He couldn't watch any more. Instead, he was facing forward and waiting for the call.

'Hand!' Nickel shouted. That was his signal.

Usain started running. He held his left arm out behind him as he started to build up speed. Nickel put the baton into his hand.

Usain looked to his left and right. He was directly in line with the USA and Japan, with Canada just behind them. It couldn't have been any closer.

He switched the baton to his right hand and – *whoosh!* – he was off. With his knees high in the air and arms pumping, he broke into full stride.

In the blink of an eye, he had opened up a one-metre gap. He knew no one could catch him now. Ever since his sports coach at primary school had told him to stop playing cricket and take up athletics, it had almost always been the same story – once he hit the front, he was unbeatable.

The race was all over long before Usain reached the finish line. Japan, the USA, Canada and the rest were blown away.

Usain was the Olympic champion again!

As he crossed the line one last time, he raised his right arm triumphantly in the air before giving a three-finger salute. One finger for each of his gold medals in Rio.

'Woooo-hoooo!'

But Usain didn't stop there. He kept on running, all the way to the Jamaican fans who were wildly waving their yellow, green and black flags in the stands. He was swallowed up in a sea of hugs.

Asafa, Yohan and Nickel quickly arrived on the scene. Cue more hugs.

'Yes, boys, we did it!'

'Jamaica, top of the world – again.'

Draped in a Jamaican flag, Usain set off with his teammates on a victory lap, but while they had run around the track in just 37.27 seconds in the relay, this lap took closer to 30 minutes this time around! Usain wanted to soak up every single second. He waved to the crowd, blew kisses and showed off some nimble footwork with his dance moves.

Finally, he gave the fans the moment they had

all been waiting for – the Lightning Bolt. It was his signature move that everyone knew. He pointed up with his left arm while keeping his right arm down, as if he was firing a bolt to the sky. The fans yelled their approval, many of them copying the pose.

There was time for one last interview.

'It's a brilliant feeling. It's been a long road. I'm happy, but I'm relieved.'

He signed off by announcing what everyone had been saying for years.

'There you go, I am the greatest.'

CHAPTER 2

ON THE MOVE

'Usain, come back here!' Jennifer cried. She had only turned her back for a few seconds but, by the time she looked around, her son had vanished.

Finally, she spotted Usain on the verandah.

'Please will you come inside to finish your lunch and sit still for just a few minutes,' she called through the window.

'Sorry, Mom,' Usain replied with a grin as he returned to the table.

A few gulps of food later, he was off again.

From the moment he was old enough to walk, Usain was on the move. Sometimes walking but, more often than not, running. In fact, he was so energetic that his parents worried that there was something wrong and took Usain to see a doctor.

'You have nothing to worry about, Mrs Bolt,' said the doctor. 'The only thing I can diagnose is that Usain is an extremely active child.'

'Oh that's a relief, isn't it, Usain?' Jennifer replied looking relieved. 'Erm, Usain…'

He was already out of the door, ready for his next adventure!

Growing up in Jamaica in the Caribbean, there was so much for the young Usain to see and explore. He lived with his parents on the north of the island, in the tiny village of Coxheath in Trelawny Parish. It was a beautiful place to live – hot, sunny and very green.

Coxheath was quiet and had a gentle pace of life, so Usain would often make his own entertainment. He loved running outside barefoot, climbing trees and messing around in the tropical forest. The best part about the forest was all the food that grew there – there were mangoes, oranges, coconuts, all kinds of exotic fruits. If Usain was ever hungry, there was always a tasty meal waiting for him a few hundred metres away.

While he was happy running around on his own, Usain could usually be found with his best friend, NJ – whose full name was Nugent Walker Junior. They met at the local school, Waldensia Primary, and spent so much time together that it wasn't long before Usain had his own nickname too. At school, he was known as 'VJ'.

The two friends were practically inseparable, both inside and outside of the classroom. Usain enjoyed some of his classes at Waldensia, particularly maths, but he soon discovered something much more interesting – cricket.

Cricket was the most popular sport on the island, and Usain – like so many of his classmates – dreamed of one day playing for the famous West Indies cricket team. His hero was Courtney Walsh, a fast bowler for the West Indies who was also from Jamaica. Usain was in awe of how quickly Courtney could bowl a cricket ball and would often pretend to be his idol when playing with NJ.

'Here comes Courtney Walsh ready to bowl. He sprints to the wicket at top speed, flings down a delivery and… he's bowled him!' Usain shouted as the ball fizzed past NJ's bat and hit the pile of stones being used as cricket stumps. He raised both arms in triumph.

'Yet another wicket for Walsh. What a terrific bowler.'

As well as cricket, Usain loved most sports and spent a lot of time at the football field near his home. He was unusually tall for a young boy and enjoyed playing as a goalkeeper, using his long limbs to keep out the shots at goal. He would throw himself around to make saves, although sometimes there would be a painful surprise waiting for him if he landed on one of the rocks hiding in the grass.

His parents encouraged Usain to take part in lots of sports, as long as they didn't get in the way of his schoolwork. They were both hard workers. Jennifer was a dressmaker, while his pops Wellesley managed a local coffee company. Wellesley would get up very early in the morning and often not come home until late at night. The rule was that Usain always had to be home before his dad returned – or there would be trouble.

One evening, Usain was playing in the forest with the family dog, Brownie. He was having so much fun that he lost track of time. Suddenly, Brownie started barking.

'What is it, boy? Have you seen a bird? Don't tell me it's a snake!'

In the distance, Usain could hear the faint sound of a motor. He looked at Brownie in horror.

'Oh no. That's Pops's motorcycle!'

With no time to lose, Usain jumped down from the tree he was climbing and ran for home as fast as he could.

'Come on, Brownie, keep up. We've got to get back before Pops.'

By the time Wellesley rode up the track to their home, Usain was sitting on the verandah with a maths book in his hands.

'Oh, hi Pops. Did you have a good day?' he said casually, in between some very deep breaths.

CHAPTER 3

FOOD FOR THOUGHT

'If you win the race, I'll buy you lunch,' said
Reverend Nugent.

Usain's ears perked up.

'And not just any lunch,' Reverend Nugent
continued, 'but jerk chicken, rice and peas.'

'You're on!' Usain replied without a moment's
hesitation. Jerk chicken was the best lunch you could
get in the whole parish of Trelawny.

Reverend Nugent was a sports coach at Waldensia
Primary. While he was very impressed with Usain's
cricket skills – both batting and bowling – what really
caught his eye was his speed when he ran in to bowl.

'Have you ever thought about taking up sprinting?'
he asked Usain after practice one day.

'No, sir.'

'Well, you should. You're easily the quickest bowler on our team. If you have some proper coaching, you could be a really good sprinter. You should enter the 100m race at the Waldensia sports day.'

Usain listened carefully to Reverend Nugent. He knew he was fast, but he wasn't the quickest runner at school – his classmate Ricardo had always beaten him.

Usain hated losing and didn't fancy losing to Ricardo again. Besides, he wanted to be a cricketer. How could he play for the West Indies if he was spending all his time focusing on sprinting? He had been planning to politely decline Reverend Nugent's suggestion – but his offer of lunch was too good to turn down.

The race would take place on the grass track at the front of Waldensia Primary. It was a straight stretch of grass, which dipped sharply just before the finish. Black lines had been burnt into the grass to separate each lane.

When Usain arrived at the school on sports day, however, he could barely see the track.

'For a small village, there sure are a lot of people here,' Usain said to himself as he stared at the hundreds and hundreds of spectators who had gathered at the side of the track, waiting for the big race. He began to feel nervous – he was desperate to put in a good performance in front of all these people.

Usain knew that if he was to have any chance of beating Ricardo, he had to start well. He was much taller than his rival, which meant it normally took him longer to get going at the start of a race. By the time he had built up full speed, Ricardo would be too far ahead.

A shout from Reverend Nugent interrupted his thoughts: 'Next race – Boys' 100m.'

Usain walked to the start line. He looked at Ricardo, who was standing to his left. Then he quickly looked away again – this wasn't the time for friendly conversation. All he wanted to do was beat him.

Usain's nerves were gone now and had been replaced by excitement. When he had run against

Ricardo previously, it had usually been friendly races after school. But this was a proper competition, a chance to win in front of a big crowd – he felt a rush of energy as the crowd fell silent before the start.

When Reverend Nugent shouted 'Go', Usain burst away from the start line with lightning-quick reactions. It was a brilliant start, much better than normal. He was already ahead of Ricardo.

Usain stretched out his long legs. After thirty metres, he was still in front but he could hear Ricardo's breathing. He ran even harder.

After a few more strides, he could no longer hear Ricardo. Instead, the only noise he could hear was the shouts from the crowd.

'Go on.'

'You can do it, VJ.'

'There's no catching him now.'

The support from the sidelines made him run even faster. He increased his lead over the final metres and broke the finishing tape to win. He was running so quickly that he fell to the ground at the finish line where the track became uneven.

But it didn't matter. Usain was the new sports day champion. He was the fastest kid at Waldensia.

'Well done, VJ,' said Ricardo after the race as he shook Usain's hand. 'You were too quick today.'

'Thanks Ricardo. That's kind of you. I'm sure it will be a great race next time.'

But deep down, Usain knew that the next time would be the same result. And the time after that. And the time after that too. Now that he had beaten Ricardo once, he was certain that he would never lose to him again.

'What did I tell you, boy? You did it!' Reverend Nugent patted Usain on the back as he offered his congratulations.

Usain smiled. It felt amazing to beat Ricardo, especially in front of so many people. He had loved the thrill of racing, but he wasn't sure if he was ready to give up on his cricketing dream just yet.

That decision could wait for now, though, as there was only one thing on Usain's mind.

'Where are we going for lunch, Reverend Nugent?'

CHAPTER 4

LEARNING CURVE

'Wake up, Usain. There's some post for you,' Jennifer said as she walked into her son's bedroom.

Usain pulled the covers over his head. 'Can't I have another ten minutes' sleep, Mom?'

'It's a letter from William Knibb Memorial High School.'

He flung the covers off straight away and sprang out of bed.

'No way. William Knibb? Do you think…?'

His voice tailed off as he ripped open the envelope and started reading the letter.

'Yes!' he yelled. 'They've offered me a scholarship.'

William Knibb Memorial High School was in Falmouth, a short drive from Usain's Coxheath home. The school was well known for its sporting success, particularly in athletics. Ever since his win over Ricardo, Usain had been unbeatable at sprinting. He was no longer just the fastest runner at Waldensia, but in the whole of Trelawny parish. And he now had plenty of trophies to prove it – the only problem was that his mom was running out of space at home to store them all!

Usain's performances and fast times had attracted the attention of the sports teachers at William Knibb school, so much so that they wanted him to come there on a sports scholarship. His parents were absolutely delighted. They were their son's biggest supporters and realised that this would be a great opportunity for his development in athletics. Without the scholarship, they would have struggled to afford to send Usain to the school.

It wasn't all good news, however. The scholarship meant Usain would have to sacrifice his first sporting love.

'The teachers believe you have the potential to become a top sprinter,' explained Wellesley. 'But that means you will have to concentrate on athletics, and only athletics. So no more cricket.'

'Could I not fit in some time for cricket after athletics training has finished, Pops?' Usain pleaded.

'I'm afraid not. The school has insisted that you must dedicate yourself completely to athletics training.'

Usain nodded. He was sad that he would have to give up on his dream to follow in Courtney Walsh's footsteps, but he understood the decision and the importance of training.

Unfortunately, when he arrived at his new school, he soon realised that training was nothing like as much fun as winning races! For starters, there was a lot of running – not just the shorter sprints that Usain was used to, but longer distances up to 1500m. They also had to do hundreds of sit-ups each day – and if any of the athletes stopped, they would all have to do them again.

Worst of all was one particularly tough drill where they would start off by running 400m. They would have a quick rest, then set off again – this time running 500m. After that, the next run would be 100m further again, and so on.

'I… am… exhausted,' Usain panted as he tried to catch his breath before the next run.

'This exercise will build up your strength and fitness for the actual races, Bolt,' came the reply from his coach. 'It's good for you.'

Usain wasn't so sure. He was easily the fastest sprinter at William Knibb – with or without any training – and would always beat his teammates over his best distances of 200m and 400m. He decided that he didn't need a serious training regime and started skipping some of the sessions.

He was also taking it easy in the classroom. While he did just enough to pass his subjects at school, that was all he did – *just* enough. He enjoyed school, but mainly the bits where he messed around with his friends, including NJ, who was also at William Knibb.

Usain loved playing pranks and jumping out on other pupils in the corridor. He also loved messing around with his friends after school, playing video games at the arcade when he should have been at training.

While some of the coaches were happy to turn a blind eye if Usain skipped a session as his times were so fast, it was a different story when his dad found out.

Wellesley was furious. He became even angrier when he discovered that his son's grades were poor as well. Usain's parents expected him to work as hard as they did.

'From now on, you'll work hard on and off the track,' Wellesley told Usain in no uncertain terms. 'I don't want to hear about any more missed training sessions.'

With those words still ringing in his ears, Usain was summoned to a meeting with William Knibb's head sports coach, Pablo McNeil.

'Not another telling off,' Usain thought as he nervously knocked on the door.

When it came to sprinting, Coach McNeil had some serious credentials. He had twice competed for Jamaica at the greatest sporting event in the world –

the Olympic Games. In Usain's mind, that meant he knew what he was talking about.

'We have a problem, Bolt,' he said. 'You're not improving.'

'But I'm the fastest runner in the school, sir.'

'Yes, you're good enough to beat everyone at this school. But are you good enough to win the regional races? Not at the moment. And the Inter-school Championships? Forget about it.'

Usain gulped.

'There's something I want to show you,' the coach continued as he turned on the video recorder in the room.

The video was from the Olympic Games in Atlanta a couple of years earlier. It showed two races – the 200m and 400m finals. Both events were won by the sprinter Michael Johnson.

Usain was spellbound as he watched the American's tall, upright frame glide smoothly around the track. He finished way ahead of all the other competitors, and in the 200m he set a new world record of 19.32 seconds. The whole stadium erupted.

'Wow, I want to be like Michael Johnson and win Olympic gold medals,' Usain said. He had found a new hero.

'Here's the thing, Usain,' Coach McNeil replied. 'You are talented enough to be an Olympic athlete one day, but you will have to work for it. Michael Johnson didn't become the star of the Olympics without years and years of training, day after day.'

This time, Usain took in every word. From that day forward, he had a new attitude to athletics.

CHAPTER 5

LIGHTNING BOLT

*'In lane five, representing William Knibb Memorial
High School... Usain Bolt.'*

A huge roar greeted the announcement of his
name. Usain looked around the stadium with his
mouth wide open. Thirty thousand spectators were
crammed into the stands. They were blowing horns,
waving flags, banging drums, and now they were
cheering his name.

He waved to where he thought his parents were
standing, but there were so many people in the
crowd that he couldn't be sure it was them.

'So this is Champs,' he said to himself, still shaking
his head. 'It's even bigger than it looks on TV.'

Champs is, to give it its full name, the Jamaican

Inter-school Championships. Each year, the best athletes from the best schools all over the island come together at the Kingston National Stadium to compete over four days. As sporting events go in Jamaica, it doesn't get much bigger. The locals love athletics, and the tickets always sell out for every day. Those not lucky enough to have a ticket can watch all the action on TV. It's that big.

In the days leading up to Champs, Coach McNeil explained to Usain just how important it was.

'Champs has been going for nearly one hundred years. All the best Jamaican athletes compete at Champs, including the great Merlene Ottey, who went on to win nine Olympic medals.'

'Nine medals? That's incredible. I'd give anything to win just one Olympic medal one day.'

'Let's concentrate on winning a medal at Champs first, Bolt!'

In fact, Usain had a chance to win not one, but two medals. He was competing in the 200m, followed by the 400m the next day.

As he stood on the starting line for the 200m final,

he was buzzing with excitement. His progress on the training programme had improved and, even though most of the boys in this under-16 event were two years older than him, he fancied his chances.

Usain had one clear – and very obvious – advantage over his rivals: his height. He had the same frame as his pops – tall and thin. He might have only been fourteen years old and not have as much muscle as others but, at six foot two, he was the tallest athlete in the race. Crucially, that meant he could take the longest strides.

The roars from the crowd grew even louder when the race started. Usain rose to the occasion, flying around the bend before hitting top speed on the final bend. He finished second, winning a silver medal.

'It's amazing to win my first Champs medal,' he said to NJ after the race, 'but now I want to turn this silver into gold.'

'I might just have the answer for you,' NJ replied, 'and it doesn't involve a magic wand.'

Usain laughed but at the same time he was keen to hear what his friend had to say. His main rival in the 400m was an athlete called Jermaine Gonzales, who would be extremely hard to beat.

'He's older than you and stronger than you, but you can beat him up here,' NJ said, pointing to his head. 'I've been watching Jermaine's races – he dominates them right from the start and leads all the way. I think if you can make a better start and get in front, then he'll panic and won't be able to catch you.'

Usain smiled. His friend had always been smart at school, and now he was showing his intelligence when it came to athletics tactics too.

The plan worked perfectly. Usain exploded out of the blocks as soon as the gun went off, working even harder than normal to get into the lead.

Just as NJ had predicted, Jermaine didn't know how to react. He tried so hard to catch Usain that he hurt his leg. The race was as good as over after 200 metres.

'Go on, son. Win it for William Knibb,' yelled Wellesley.

'That's my boy,' cried Jennifer as Usain cruised home to the finish.

The horns blared as he crossed the line first. He was the new 400m champion!

It was an incredible feeling. 'I could get used to this,' Usain thought as he received his gold medal later that afternoon.

In the weeks and months that followed, there were many more opportunities for him to win medals, at many more regional and national events. Most exciting of all was the chance to compete in the Bahamas the following year, when he was fifteen.

'You've been selected to represent Jamaica in the CARIFTA Games,' Coach McNeil told Usain.

'Excuse me, the CARI-what?'

'It's short for the Caribbean Free Trade Association. It's a huge athletics meeting for the best young athletes in the whole Caribbean, from more than twenty different countries.'

Usain was one of sixty-four Jamaican athletes who flew to the Bahamas for the event. He was so excited to represent his country, but even more excited to be on a plane.

'This thing goes even faster than I do,' he shouted as the plane took off.

Usain was so proud to pull on the yellow, green and black vest of Jamaica. He always wanted to win every race he competed in, but wearing the national colours made him even hungrier for victory. As soon as he hit the track, there was no stopping him.

The 200m? A new CARIFTA record of 21.12, finishing nearly a second ahead of his teammate Andre Wellington.

The 400m? A new CARIFTA record of 47.33, and this time he was even further ahead of the second-placed runner: more than 1.5 seconds.

By the time the 4x400m relay came around, which Usain ran with three Jamaican teammates, the whole crowd knew who he was. He was one of the stars of the Games and he didn't disappoint in his third and final event.

As he collected the baton from his teammate before he set off on the final leg, Usain was in first place, ahead of the Bahamas and Grenada.

'I'll give the fans something to savour,' he thought as he quickly extended his lead.

But hang on a minute, what was that noise?

There was a low murmur coming from the crowd.

Usain strained to hear what they were saying, while simultaneously trying to concentrate on completing the race without dropping the baton.

The murmur grew louder.

Finally, as he raised his arms triumphantly at the end of the race, he worked out what everyone was singing.

'Bolt! Bolt! Lightning Bolt!'

'Bolt! Bolt! Lightning Bolt!'

Usain had won three gold medals, he had set three CARIFTA records, and now he had a new nickname too.

CHAPTER 6

WORLD BEATER

Usain raised his eyebrows as he scanned the list in front of him. There were so many different countries – Germany, Ireland, Belgium and Madagascar, to name just a few.

'Yo, Jermaine, this guy's from Kazakhstan. I don't even know what continent that's on!'

His teammate Jermaine Gonzales came over with a big grin on his face.

'Don't you worry about all the other competitors, Usain,' he said. 'There's only one person that matters in this race – and that's you.'

Usain smiled. 'Thanks for the advice,' he said, before adding, 'But seriously, man – Kazakhstan?'

The piece of paper that had grabbed Usain's

attention was the start list for his next 200m race. Not just any 200m race, but the first-round heat of the 2002 World Junior Championships.

Held every two years, the championships attracted the best athletes aged under twenty from all over the planet. In 2002, more than 1,000 athletes were competing, from over 150 countries. As luck would have it, the event was taking place practically on Usain's doorstep – at the National Stadium in Kingston. That made this competition even more special.

Usain loved competing in the big events and having the chance to meet other athletes from all around the world. Plus it meant he could miss school for a few days too!

Unlike the CARIFTA Games, Usain and Jermaine would not be going head-to-head in the 400m. Coach McNeil had decided that Usain's best chance of winning a medal would be to focus solely on the 200m. It was his strongest individual event and his times had been improving all year. Usain was more than happy with his coach's decision – the 400m could be really hard work!

The World Junior Championships was by some margin the biggest competition that Usain had competed in so far. He was so excited to compete for Jamaica against all these other countries in front of his home fans, but at the same time there was another nagging feeling building up inside him.

He was nervous.

'What if I don't perform well in front of the fans?' he worried in the days leading up to the 200m. 'My race is going to be shown on TV all around the world – what if I mess it up?'

He tried to relax by playing video games with NJ or watching football on TV, but nothing worked. It didn't help that he was three or even four years younger than so many of the athletes. At fifteen, he was one of the youngest competitors at the whole championships, which meant his body was less developed. He stared in awe at the muscles of some of his rivals. 'Those arms are wider than my legs!'

Despite their size, though, Usain's fellow

competitors still had to look up to him. Now an astonishing six foot five, he was the tallest sprinter in the event.

As soon as the gun sounded to start Usain's heat, his worries evaporated. He scorched around the track, stopping the clock at 20.58. It was only when he spoke to Coach McNeil later that he realised quite how fast he had run.

'How does it feel to be the fastest fifteen-year-old on the planet, Bolt?'

Usain had broken the world record! It was the quickest ever time for someone his age over 200m.

Coach McNeil still wasn't happy, though.

'You never saw Michael Johnson breaking the world record in his heat, boy. He would do enough to get through the rounds and save his best time for the final.'

With those words fresh in his mind, Usain ran a smarter race in the semi-final. He didn't give 100 per cent effort, but still did enough to take first place.

He had qualified for his first world final.

As the hours slowly ticked down to the biggest

race of his life, the familiar nervous feelings returned. Usain was the fastest qualifier for the final, and the Jamaican fans were getting very excited at the prospect of their athlete winning gold.

Only on entering the National Stadium did Usain realise quite how excited the fans were. The noise was deafening. People were playing trumpets and thumping drums – it was like a Caribbean carnival had gathered inside the stadium.

'All these people are supporting me,' Usain thought. 'I don't want to let them down.'

The pressure was getting to him. He knew he needed to block all the noise out and concentrate on his race, but he couldn't. Besides, it was difficult to ignore 30,000 people chanting his name.

'Bolt, Bolt, Lightning Bolt!'

Even the simplest task was proving tricky. With minutes to go before the start of the race, he couldn't put his running spikes on.

'Why won't this shoe fit?' he snapped as he tried and failed again to put it on his left foot.

He began to panic.

'Has someone swapped my spikes? This is a really bad joke.'

Finally, he realised his mistake. He was trying to put his right shoe on his left foot.

'How am I going to win a world title if I can't even put my spikes on?' he groaned.

He managed to get ready just as the stadium announcer gave his starting orders.

Usain was in lane 3. Immediately to his right was the American Wes Felix. Brendan Christian, from Antigua and Barbuda, was another big threat in lane 6. As the gun sounded, all the athletes powered out of the blocks. All of them except Usain, that is. He had frozen.

It was a terrible start. By the time he eventually got away, he was at least a metre behind his rivals. He couldn't believe he'd made such a bad mistake. However, he didn't have any time to worry about that now – instead, he flung his arms with all his might as he set about closing the gap.

The louder the fans cheered, the faster Usain ran, and as he came around the bend with 100m to go, he was up to third. Brendan still led by a metre.

Soon, third became second as he edged ahead of Wes. With eighty metres to go, he drew level with Brendan. The fans were going berserk. Two big strides later, he was in front, and once he took the lead, there was no stopping him. His advantage kept increasing all the way to the finish.

At the line, Usain was four metres ahead of the rest of the field. He had come from eighth to first. It was the best race of his life.

'Wooo-hooo!' yelled the new world junior 200m champion.

'Bolt, Bolt, Lightning Bolt!' the crowd screamed.

Usain had done it. Gold for Jamaica. And he knew it wouldn't have been possible without the incredible support from the stands. As he jogged around the stadium on his lap of honour, he wanted to thank the fans for believing in him. He posed for photos, signed autographs and even gave them a salute.

One of the spectators chucked a Jamaican flag onto the track. Usain picked it up and wore it as a cape, just as he had seen his hero Michael Johnson do at the Olympics.

It was the greatest win of Usain's life and he didn't want the moment to ever end.

CHAPTER 7

ALL WORK, NO PLAY

'VJ, come here please.'

Usain frowned as he heard his pops's voice. He slowly got up from the chair on the verandah, wondering what he might have done wrong.

'Now!'

That made him move a lot faster. Wellesley had always been firm but fair with his son – and from the sound of his voice, Usain could tell he was going to be very firm right now.

'I had an interesting phone call with your teacher today…' he said while waving a letter in his hand.

Usain sighed. Whatever was on that piece on paper wasn't good news.

'…about your grades.'

Usain's heart sank. This really wasn't good news.

Life had changed for Usain ever since his World Junior Championships success. At fifteen years and 332 days, he had become the youngest ever junior world champion, and suddenly everyone seemed to know who he was. His face had been on the front and back pages of all the Jamaican newspapers. He was invited to lots of events and parties. People kept coming up to chat to him at school or in the street.

With so much going on, plus the need to keep training hard and focusing on athletics, Usain had found there wasn't much time left for his schoolwork, and his grades had suffered as a result.

But his dad wasn't interested in any excuses.

'You might be the fastest fifteen-year-old in the world, but you need some help to improve your grades. We have decided to hire a tutor for you.'

'Come on, Pops. I promise I'll try harder at school. We don't need to waste a poor tutor's time looking after me,' Usain pleaded, realising that having a tutor would mean more time studying and less time having fun.

But it was no use.

'You'll start your first class with Mr Peart tomorrow evening.'

And that was that. For two or three evenings a week, Mr Peart would come to Usain's home and teach him English, maths and any other subjects that needed his attention. As much as Usain disliked the extra lessons, he got on well with his tutor, who was a big athletics fan and had been a good 800m runner himself.

'Running around the whole track once is too far for me, Mr Peart, let alone the 800m!' Usain joked. He enjoyed listening to his tutor talk about his running days and learned some valuable tips on how to juggle his schoolwork with training.

On the track at least, Usain continued to produce A-grade results, particularly in the 200m. In 2003, he won the World Youth Championships in Canada. Coach McNeil wanted him to double up and run the

400m, but Usain hated that distance almost as much as being stuck inside studying.

In Canada, he took drastic measures to avoid competing, pretending that he had a stomach bug. The Jamaican coaching team weren't so sure and made him go to the doctor for a check-up. In order to 'prove' he was telling the truth, Usain then had to sit in the bathroom for what seemed like hours. He was bored out of his mind, but it was worth it – there would be no 400m.

After another successful championships, it was decision time for Usain. In order to take the next step in his development, he would need to leave William Knibb Memorial High School and dedicate himself full-time to athletics.

Thanks to Mr Peart's help, Usain passed five subjects which meant, if he wanted, he could attend any of the top sports colleges in America, where many of the best young athletes trained. But while he realised he couldn't stay in Coxheath all his life, he didn't want to move abroad.

Usain loved Jamaica, his family, the people,

hanging out with NJ and other friends, the relaxed way of life, the warm weather and – although he would never dare tell his pops – all the parties!

After talking with his parents, it was decided that he would move to the High Performance Centre in Kingston. And to stop his mom from worrying and to ensure he stayed out of trouble, Mr Peart would go with him.

They shared an apartment together in Kingston, so although Mr Peart was no longer teaching Usain, he was always on hand to give advice. He also had a very smart business brain and became Usain's manager.

The centre was a different world from William Knibb school – it was one of the best athletics clubs in the whole of Jamaica. Usain had full-time coaching all day, every day, and could devote all his time to the track without ever having to worry about handing in his homework.

That's not to say it wasn't tough, though. His new athletics teacher, Coach Coleman, was a hard taskmaster.

'Bolt, fifty press-ups. Now!'

'Bolt, run 400m at full speed. Go!'

'Too slow! Do another 400. Actually, let's make it 500.'

And even when the track training was finally over for the day, Usain would have to go to the gym to lift weights.

He was exhausted, so much so that he longed for the old days at William Knibb school.

'I can't believe I'm saying this, but I think I want Coach McNeil back,' he told Mr Peart one evening.

'This training is all part of your development, Usain. It's a huge step up from the junior championships to becoming a professional athlete. You'll be competing against sprinters almost twice your age. They're twice as experienced and twice as strong. The only way to get to their level is through hard work.'

Usain nodded. 'I know, Mr Peart, but this is *really* hard work,' he moaned.

'Well, it will all be worth it if you run for Jamaica in the Athens Olympics next year.'

Usain's mood was instantly lifted by that thought.

CHAPTER 8

GREEK TRAGEDY

'Aaarrrggghhh!'

Usain let out a blood-curdling scream as he collapsed on the track. It felt like someone had stabbed him in the back of his leg.

It had been another regular training session in Kingston, which meant running lots and lots of laps. For months on end, Usain had been telling Coach Coleman – and anyone within earshot – that his training programme was doing more harm than good. He knew that all this strength training wasn't good for his body. Even though he was running fast times, something didn't feel right. But no one had listened to his concerns.

And now it was too late.

On this particular drill, Usain had been told
to sprint a series of 400m laps as fast as he
could. Halfway round the track, he felt the most
excruciating pain in his thigh, which made him fall
to the ground.

After a couple of minutes of lying motionless, he
tried to get up again. Maybe it was just cramp and it
was better now?

'Aaaaarrrrrgggggghhhhh!'

It was even more painful than before. Usain
slumped back to the ground. He couldn't walk.

'Why now?' he mumbled as he was helped off the
track by the coaching staff. The injury couldn't have
come at a worse time.

Just a few weeks earlier, Usain had broken the
junior world record for the 200m with a wonderful
run of 19.93 seconds. Not only that, but no one,
junior or senior, had run a faster time in 2004. All the
papers were saying that he was a certainty to win the
World Junior Championships again in the summer
and, even more excitingly, that he could win a medal
at the Athens Olympic Games a month later.

He had long dreamed of standing on the podium in a packed stadium with an Olympic medal hanging around his neck – just like Michael Johnson had done. But now Usain didn't know if he would even make it to Athens, let alone challenge for the medals.

Over the next few weeks, Usain became very familiar with what a medical room looked like, as a succession of doctors and physios tried to help him recover. It was an incredibly frustrating time. All he wanted to do was be out on the track, but that was the one thing he couldn't do. He was ordered to stay still – something he hadn't done since he was a baby!

'You can't run before you can walk, Bolt,' Coach Coleman said.

'I understand, coach, but I'm not even allowed to walk right now!' Usain replied, half-smiling.

Eventually, after a long period of recuperation, the verdict was in.

'There's good news and there's bad news,' Coach Coleman said to Usain one morning. 'Which do you want first?'

'Please just put me out of my misery, coach.' Usain was in no mood for games. It was too serious.

'Okay, the doctors have said that you won't be fit enough for the World Junior Championships, but you should be able to go to Athens.'

Usain didn't know whether to laugh or cry. Defending his world junior title had been his main goal for the season – he was devastated to miss out on that opportunity. But there was still the Olympics. Olympic gold was the most treasured prize in all of athletics, and the Games only came around every four years. Usain may have only been seventeen, but he realised he had to grab his chance.

It was a race against time to get fit, and – as was so often the case – he won the race. He was selected to represent Jamaica in the 200m.

Deep down, though, Usain was worried when he arrived in Athens. He should have been over the moon to be at the world's greatest sporting event, but he couldn't enjoy himself. His body was still recovering and he wasn't in anything like as good form as earlier in the season. When he was confident, Usain felt he could beat anyone on the planet. However, that confidence hadn't made the trip with him to the Olympics.

Two days before the 200m heats were due to start, Usain sat down to watch the world's fastest men compete in the Olympic 100m final. It was a good chance to check out his rivals, many of whom would be competing in his event in forty-eight hours. He also wanted to cheer on his Jamaican teammate Asafa Powell.

However, there was one man who caught his eye above everyone else.

At six foot one, Justin Gatlin was four inches shorter than Usain, but he certainly had a big presence on the track – and even bigger celebrations when he won.

'I'd like to go head-to-head against him,' Usain thought as he watched Gatlin outsprint everyone to win 100m gold. 'You might have beaten Asafa tonight, but I'll get revenge for Jamaica one day.'

It was far too hot to think about revenge, or indeed pretty much anything else, when Usain lined up for his 200m heat a couple of days later. The weather was sweltering – even for a Jamaican.

All Usain's worries and fears came to life when the gun sounded. His legs felt tired and as hard as he moved his arms, he couldn't go any faster – it was as if he was running in mud. He could only watch helplessly as the other runners sprinted away from him. On his best form, he would easily have won the heat. Instead, he finished fifth and didn't qualify for the quarter-finals.

It was no consolation the following evening when Usain watched Shawn Crawford of the USA win gold and realised that his time earlier in the season of 19.93 would have been good enough for a silver medal. That only made him more frustrated about the injury and the training programme.

'You're still very young and have plenty of time on your hands,' Asafa said as he tried to lift Usain's mood after the final.

'Things will be very different at the Beijing Olympics in four years' time, believe me,' Usain vowed.

CHAPTER 9

A NEW REGIME

This wasn't how the Olympics had panned out in Usain's dreams. He just wanted to get out of Greece and fly back to Jamaica. And he was determined that things would change when he got home. First on the list was finding a new coach.

Usain had a good feeling as soon as he walked into the Racers Track Club. The place was full of energy. There were some athletes stretching, some athletes doing warm-up jogs, and other athletes deep in conversation with their coaches.

'It makes a change from everyone running the 400m again and again,' he said to himself with a sigh of relief.

Suddenly, a booming voice made him jump.

'Come on, boy, you're not going to become the Olympic champion just by watching everyone else!'

Usain spun around to see the grinning face of Glen Mills. This was his new coach.

'Pleased to meet you, Coach Mills,' Usain replied with a smile.

'You too, Bolt. Now, before we start, I'd like to have a chat about your programme and what you think will work best for you.'

That sounded good to Usain.

Coach Mills was different from any of his previous coaches. Coaching was a two-way thing. He explained his thoughts and what he believed worked best for Usain, and then would listen to what Usain had to say.

The coach was also very experienced and had trained many of the world's leading athletes, including Kim Collins, the sprinter from the Caribbean islands of St Kitts and Nevis who won 100m gold at the 2003 World Championships.

It was for these reasons that Usain had chosen

to join Coach Mills's team and move to the Racers Track Club just outside Kingston.

'You're a very talented athlete, Bolt, but – to make the most of your talents – we need to build up your fitness and your body so you can cope with the demands of being a professional sprinter. This will take time. We are going to work on a plan to win gold at the Beijing Olympics in 2008.'

'2008?' Usain replied in shock. 'That's three years away! What are we going to do in between?'

Coach Mills laughed. 'All in good time, Bolt. You must be patient. You're only eighteen years old.'

Over the months that followed, Usain learned about everything he needed to do to become a top athlete. He learned about diet, the things he should eat, and the things that were bad for him and he had to avoid: 'Pretty much everything I like!' He learned how to look after his body through physio and stretching every day – legs, arms, back, everything. He learned about the importance of warming up properly before he ran, so his muscles wouldn't be cold and tighten up.

There was a lot to learn, but Usain was a keen student – and much keener than he had been at the William Knibb classroom!

There was still a lot of jogging, running and sprinting to be done too, of course, as part of his training. And when he left the club at the end of the day, Usain's work still wasn't finished. Coach Mills gave him a long list of exercises to do each evening at home and, to make sure Usain did them, he often turned up on his doorstep!

'Come on, coach. Can't I have a night off and have some fun for once?' Usain begged.

'Here's a solution, Bolt. Why don't you do your sit-ups while watching Manchester United play on the TV?'

Much as he enjoyed watching Premier League football and his beloved Manchester United, that didn't sound like a lot of fun to Usain.

As tiring as his new regime was, Usain was in high spirits by the time the World Championships in Helsinki came around in 2005. His legs felt strong, his muscles were bulging, and he was raring to go.

'The Beijing Olympics are our main goal, Bolt,' said Coach Mills, 'but the World Championships will be a great experience for you. You need to learn how to run and manage your body at a championship. If you are to reach the 200m final, you will have to run four races in three days.'

'What's your advice, Coach?'

'We don't want a repeat of what happened in Athens. You need to run hard enough to make sure you qualify for the next round, but not too hard.'

Usain grimaced at the memory of his first Olympics a year earlier. He listened carefully to his coach's words and was determined to follow his advice.

There was one thing he couldn't prepare for, however – the weather in Finland. It was very cold and very wet.

'I thought it was meant to be summer,' Usain said, shivering as he tried to warm up for his first heat. 'Imagine what it's like in winter here.'

Things quickly heated up when he hit the track. After winning his heat, he finished second in the quarter-final, then fourth in the semi-final, which was just enough to qualify for the final. The only setback was that, since he was one of the slowest qualifiers, he was drawn in lane 1 for the final. Lane 1, on the inside of the running track, had a very tight bend, which made it tricky for athletes as tall as Usain to run the start of the race aggressively. Another reason why he enjoyed the middle lanes was that he could be in the thick of the action between his rivals.

Still, nothing could dampen his excitement ahead of his first major final. It was a high-class field and there were four American stars in the race. One name jumped out at Usain immediately: Justin Gatlin.

Gatlin had already won the 100m gold and was very confident that he would win the double. Usain wasn't sure if he could stop him, but he thought he might have a chance of a medal if he ran really well.

The evening of the 200m final was even colder and wetter than the previous days. Usain simply could not get warm. He was not helped by the fact that there were several delays to the race and a false start, which meant more time waiting around.

At last, the gun went. Usain made a great start. Despite being in lane 1, he flew around the bend and was level with Gatlin as they entered the final 100m. As the older, more experienced sprinters started to edge ahead, Usain pushed really hard to keep up with them.

Too hard.

There was a sudden pain in his leg. He had to stop running at full speed. His muscles had been too cold and had tightened – just as Coach Mills had warned him in training. As he slowed down, he was determined to finish the race, even though his leg was really hurting. He jogged to the line, coming in six seconds behind the victorious Gatlin and the rest of the field.

As Usain trudged off the track, he watched Gatlin celebrate with his USA teammates and wave the American flag in the air. It didn't improve his mood and only made him want to win even more next time.

He was surprised to see the smiling face of Coach Mills waiting for him.

'Well done, Bolt.'

'What do you mean, Coach? I came last.'

'Yes, but you were matching the best athletes in the world. Then, when you got injured, you proved your determination and courage by finishing the race.'

Those words made the pain of losing a little easier for Usain to stomach.

CHAPTER 10

SILVER LINING

'Bolt, you've proved you have the ability. You've proved you've got the heart. Now the next challenge is to prove you can do it when it really matters – in a major championship.'

Coach Mills was talking to Usain after another tough training session. Over the previous year, Usain's training had gone from strength to strength. There had been no major championships in 2006, so the main focus had been to continue his development and minimise the chances of further injury problems.

But it wasn't all work and no play. Just as Usain had never let his schoolwork get in the way of having a good time, he loved messing around away from the Racers Track Club. While some of his rivals led very boring lives, dedicated to athletics twenty-four hours a day, Usain was made of different stuff. He needed to have fun.

Living in the big city and bright lights of Kingston was a completely different world from that of the quiet village of Coxheath. There was so much to see and do – day and night. His favourite pastime was to go dancing in Kingston's clubs with NJ and his other friends. He was always practising some crazy new dance move. It was a great way to let off steam after training.

However, while Coach Mills didn't mind his star pupil going out once in a while, he put his foot down if he thought it was getting in the way of his athletics commitments.

'Bolt, you're spending more time on the dance floor than on the training track.'

'Come on, Coach, it's good for me. You should see how hard I work while I'm dancing – I sweat buckets.'

'If you had half as much dedication to sprinting as you do to dancing, you'd run the 200m in 18 seconds! You can go out partying as much as you like when you're the Olympic champion, but until then you need to knuckle down.'

With the 2007 World Championships in Osaka just around the corner, Usain got the message: it was time to get to work. If he could bring his best form to Japan, there was every chance he could win a medal, especially as one of his major rivals wouldn't be there.

A year earlier it had been announced that Justin Gatlin had been found guilty of cheating to improve his performance. As punishment, he was banned from competing for eight years.

Usain was lost for words when he found out. He couldn't believe that any athlete would resort to cheating to try to win. He was desperate to be the best, but only by playing fair, through his own talent and hard work – never by cheating. And if another athlete ran faster on the day, then the only option was to accept it – and try even harder to beat him the next time.

With Gatlin absent, another American – Tyson Gay – was the man to beat in Osaka. He had already run the 200m in 19.62 seconds that season. Usain could only dream of a time like that.

Tyson wasn't just speedy over 200m; he was rapid at 100m too. In the final in Osaka, he beat Usain's teammate Asafa Powell to win gold, which really made Usain take notice, as Asafa was the 100m world record holder.

'Watch out for the last thirty metres, Usain,' Asafa warned. 'He gets even quicker as the race goes on.'

Usain couldn't think too far ahead yet, though. First, he had to make sure he qualified for the final. After cruising through his first heat, he won the next two rounds without using up too much energy – just as Coach Mills had instructed him. That meant he was drawn in lane 5 for the final, right in the thick of the action and sandwiched between Tyson Gay and his USA teammate Wallace Spearmon Jr.

Usain was pumped up. There were no nerves or cold weather to disrupt him this time. He waved to the fans as his name was announced. He sped out of the blocks and was the quickest athlete around the bend. Tyson was so close to him that he could hear his breathing and the sound of his spikes hitting the track but, crucially, Usain was in the lead.

The finish line was only ninety metres away. 'Could this be my moment?' he thought.

Then, out of the corner of his eye, he suddenly spotted the figure wearing the white and red of the USA. Tyson drew alongside him. Usain strained to keep up, but it was no use. The American increased his lead all the way to the finish. Asafa had been right about those final thirty metres!

Usain had mixed emotions as he crossed the line. A silver medal was an amazing achievement and he had finally delivered at a major championship, but it wasn't the colour of medal he really wanted.

As soon as the race was over, he gave Tyson a hug. His parents had always taught him to be polite and well-mannered, and Usain insisted on showing respect to his fellow competitors.

'How come Tyson was so much faster at the end of the race?' he asked Coach Mills later that evening.

'Because he's stronger than you, Bolt. If you want to win in Beijing, you need to push yourself even harder.'

CHAPTER 11

FASTEST MAN ON EARTH

Usain crouched down on the starting blocks. Immediately to his right was Tyson Gay, so close that Usain could hear his every breath. It would be the first time he had ever raced his American rival over the 100m.

In fact, this meeting in New York would be only the fifth time Usain had run the 100m as a professional athlete. For the past couple of years, he had been locked in a running argument with Coach Mills, who wanted him to compete in another event in addition to the 200m. Coach Mills's preference was the 400m.

'Come on, coach, the 400m is way too far. I need to make the most of my speed over a shorter distance, like the 100m,' Usain said. He had never enjoyed running the 400m – it was exhausting and hurt a lot!

'But there's no room for error over the 100m, Bolt. One mistake and you're out of it. Plus you need a great start, which is hard for you because you're so tall.'

The argument raged on and on until they finally made a deal that Usain would do a one-off 100m race. If he ran well, he would compete in the 100m in 2008. If not, it would be the 400m. The thought of a season of pain was more than enough motivation for Usain, and he produced a rapid run of 10.03 in his debut 100m. The time was so quick that it even surprised Coach Mills, who had no choice but to grant Usain his wish.

And so, here he was in New York, ready to test himself against the man who had beaten him in Osaka. Forget about tall men being slow out of the blocks, on the 'b' of the bang of the gun Usain accelerated away with the ferocity of a Formula One car. Tyson was seven inches shorter than Usain and known for his fast starts, but he was instantly left trailing.

Usain drove on, determined to extend his lead. This was where his height was an advantage – with his longer legs, he needed to take far fewer strides than Tyson. His knees were going so high they almost came up to his chest.

As they approached the final thirty metres, Usain wondered if Tyson would fight back, just like he had done in Osaka. But all the hard work on the training track was paying off. He was hitting top form in 2008 just like Coach Mills had planned. Usain was stronger than ever before and, if anything, he increased his lead over Tyson at the finish.

Usain raised both arms in celebration as he crossed the line. He was so excited that he didn't slow down and kept running around the track, thumping his chest with joy. It showed how much it meant to him to win.

The noise from the crowd was almost ear-splitting. Even though they were in the USA, Usain had strong support in the stands, as lots of Jamaicans lived in

New York. But it sounded like the whole of Jamaica was in the stadium.

'How come everyone is getting *so* excited?' Usain thought as he looked around to see spectators on their feet and punching the air.

Then he saw the official race time and it dawned on him.

9.72.

Surely not? He looked again to make sure.

There it was, the official time: 9.72 seconds.

Usain had broken the 100m world record!

His jaw dropped in disbelief. All he had been thinking about was beating Tyson; the time hadn't even entered his head. No wonder everyone was so excited – he was officially the fastest man on earth.

'Wooo-hooo!'

He let out a massive scream and the crowd became even more excited.

When the celebrations eventually died down, Usain felt a tap on his shoulder. It was Tyson.

'Well done, Usain. That was a brilliant run.'

'Thanks Tyson. It was a great race.'

That night, Usain struggled to sleep as he couldn't stop thinking about his world record. The words from the commentary were running around his head.

'Usain Bolt takes the 100m. It's a new world record. 9.72. Usain Bolt has run the fastest 100m in the history of humankind.'

In less than three months, he would go to the Olympics in Beijing, not only with high hopes in the 200m, but as the quickest 100m runner on the whole planet.

The argument with Coach Mills had been settled once and for all.

CHAPTER 12

BEIJING BRILLIANCE

'This place is incredible,' Usain said to Asafa Powell, as they walked around the Olympic Village in Beijing. For the next two weeks, this village – built specially for the athletes – would be Usain's home.

The village accommodated nearly 11,000 athletes in all, as well as their coaching and support staff, and with so many people staying there, Usain just blended into the crowd. It made a nice change not to stand out as the tallest athlete for once – he was dwarfed by Chinese basketball legend Yao Ming, who was more than a foot taller than him!

Athletics was just one part of the Olympic Games – there were a total of 28 different sports and more than 300 gold medals to be won.

'I'd be happy to win just one or two golds,' Usain thought, completely stunned by the size of the whole event.

He loved the Olympic Village. He was staying in an apartment block with the Jamaican team and, in the days leading up to the athletics competition, he would relax with his friends, playing video games or dominoes. He often stayed up late chatting with his teammates, much to the annoyance of Coach Mills whose bedroom was next door.

Despite all the fun, Usain didn't forget about home completely. His mom and Mr Peart were both coming out to Beijing to watch him race, and he would regularly call Pops and NJ back home to give them all the latest news.

One of the regular topics of conversation was the food. Usain wasn't a big fan of the Chinese cuisine, so his diet mainly consisted of chicken nuggets from the McDonald's restaurant in the village. Breakfast, lunch and dinner were all the same – another box of nuggets. 'Best not to let Coach Mills know about this!' Usain thought with a smile.

Usain was in a confident mood when the first day of the 100m arrived. The athletics events were taking place in the Olympic Stadium, which everyone called the Bird's Nest – as that was exactly what it looked like!

'Let's give everyone something to crow about,' Usain said to himself as he waved to the crowd. He coasted through the first two rounds, qualifying easily for the next day, which would see the semi-final and the final.

The day of the final was very hot. Coach Mills made sure Usain drank lots of water to keep hydrated. After winning his semi-final, there was no time to return to the village before the final, so Usain hung out at the warm-up track. One of his main rivals would be Asafa, who had held the world record before Usain's blistering run in New York. Tyson Gay had been struggling with an injury and didn't make the final.

But Usain didn't care who else was in the race. He was so relaxed, chatting with Coach Mills and the physios. It was just like another day at training – not the Olympic 100m final!

He even pulled a prank on Coach Mills on live
TV. The cameras were filming Usain as he received
a massage from his physio. When Coach Mills came
over and put a hand on his shoulder, he collapsed to
the floor in fake agony, pretending that his coach had
injured him.

Coach Mills didn't see the funny side of it.

'Less messing about please, Bolt – you've got a
final to concentrate on.'

Nevertheless, his coach was happy to see Usain so
calm and not showing any signs of nerves before the
biggest race of his life. The 100m final wasn't just
the most popular event in athletics; it was the most
important event in the whole Olympics and known
as the 'blue riband' race since it decided the fastest
runner in the world.

The fun continued in the call room, where the
athletes waited before entering the stadium for the
start of the race. For some, it was a chance to try to
intimidate the other competitors – staring at them,
shouting, even banging the walls. Not Usain, though
– he was too busy having fun. As well as Asafa,

there were four other runners from the Caribbean in the final. Usain messed around with all of them, cracking jokes.

When he walked out onto the track, he was just as calm – right up to the very start of the race. When athletes are introduced by the stadium announcer, they are usually very serious and focused, concentrating on the race ahead, but Usain was fooling around for the TV cameras, rubbing his hair and smiling for the whole world to see.

He couldn't have been more relaxed and he didn't even panic when he made a slow start in lane 3. After twenty-five metres, he was level with the leaders, then started to pull away from everyone at the halfway point. He kept powering further and further ahead. It was like he was in a different race from everyone else.

With thirty metres left, Usain looked around and knew he wouldn't be caught. He started waving his arms in celebration, even though the race wasn't over. He eased down at the finish and, just as he had done in New York, kept running around the whole track. He didn't even notice that he had broken the world record again or that his shoelace had come undone during the race.

Finally, he stopped. As the crowd roared their approval, he pointed his arms skywards as if he was an archer firing a lightning bolt into the air. It was a spur-of-the-moment celebration.

The next few minutes were a blur as Usain performed a lap of honour, stopping for photos, autographs and high-fiving the fans. He was desperate to see his mom and Mr Peart, but didn't think there'd be any chance of finding them among so many people, who were all calling out his name.

But then he heard a familiar cry.

'Hey, VJ, over here. VJ!'

Only people from Coxheath called him VJ. He looked up to see his mom and Mr Peart waving wildly in the stands, and ran to give them a big hug.

'That's my boy – the Olympic champion!'

'Great race, VJ. We're so proud of you.'

It was the greatest moment of Usain's life. He had achieved his dream of winning an Olympic gold medal.

He was still buzzing when he returned to his room at the Olympic Village that night.

There was a knock on the door. It was Coach Mills.

'So, are you happy we chose to run the 100m, Coach?' Usain asked with a chuckle.

'It was a brilliant run, Bolt, but I just have one question.'

'What's that?'

'Why did you slow down at the end? You could have run even faster.'

Usain smiled. There was never any pleasing Coach Mills.

CHAPTER 13

LIGHTNING STRIKES AGAIN

'Can I have your autograph please?'

'Will you pose for a photo with me?'

'Hey Usain, do the Lightning Bolt.'

After his 100m win, life in the Olympic Village was turned upside down for Usain. He was no longer just another face in the crowd – everyone knew who he was and wanted to say hi.

As much as Usain enjoyed meeting other athletes, though, sometimes it got a bit overwhelming. He couldn't even go to get some chicken nuggets without someone wanting to do the Lightning Bolt with him.

Plus his Olympics weren't over yet. He still had the 200m to focus on, and then the relay. While the 100m had been a relatively new challenge for Usain, the 200m had always been his main event – and he had been planning for this race ever since hooking up with Coach Mills three years earlier.

Following his world record in the 100m final, a lot of people were wondering if Usain could repeat the feat in his favourite event.

Usain wasn't so sure. He knew he was in top form, but the 200m world record was 19.32 seconds, far quicker than he'd ever run before. What's more, his hero Michael Johnson still held the record from that magical run at the Olympics 12 years earlier, which had so inspired Usain. Michael had beaten the second-placed athlete by a huge margin of 0.36 seconds. Usain didn't know if anyone could *ever* run that fast again.

He received an enormous reception from the Bird's Nest crowd before the start of the 200m final. His 100m win had made headlines all over the world, and he didn't disappoint the fans when his name was announced. He danced around with his hands, rubbing his hair, and performed the now famous Lightning Bolt. It gave Usain a real thrill to excite the crowd and also took away any nerves.

Not that he needed to worry. By the halfway point of the final, Usain was so far ahead it felt like a one-man race. Now he was running against the clock.

Unlike a few nights earlier, he didn't relax as he approached the finish but made sure he kept pushing. He lunged his head forward at the line to stop the clock.

Usain looked at the time. 19.30 seconds.

He had beaten Michael Johnson's record!

Usain threw his arms out in celebration. Then he collapsed to the track, with arms and legs stretched wide like a starfish as he stared at the sky. No wonder he was tired – it was an incredible time. He had won the race by a massive 0.66 seconds.

When he finally caught his breath, Usain was in the mood to celebrate with the fans. He did the Lightning Bolt, and all the fans did it back to him. Someone chucked a Jamaican flag onto the track. He quickly wrapped it around his shoulders – he was so proud to win for his country. Then he took off his spikes and started pulling out some of the dance moves that he had practised in the Kingston clubs. The crowd had never seen anything like this before.

Usain was the new entertainer of athletics.

As well as all the congratulations from fans, friends and family, there was one comment that really stood out. Michael Johnson called him 'Superman II'. He described it as 'an incredible time, an incredible performance'. It meant so much to Usain to hear those words from his idol.

Michael had won two gold medals at the Atlanta Olympics. Now Usain wanted to go one step better and make it a hat-trick of golds in the 4x100m relay. He loved the relay as it was a chance to compete with his Jamaican teammates, rather than against them. And in Nesta Carter, Michael Frater and Asafa Powell, Jamaica had an awesome team.

Nesta would start off, handing the baton to Michael, who in turn would pass it to Usain. The final leg would be run by Asafa. There was one small problem, however.

'Yo, we forgot to practise the baton handovers,' said Michael before the final. 'It's too late now. What if we drop the baton?'

Usain had been relaxed throughout the whole Olympics and saw no need to start worrying now.

'Don't worry, bro,' he replied, putting an arm around his teammate. 'We've got the four fastest runners in the race. Let's just get the baton around safely, not take any risks, and we'll be fine.'

As it turned out, they were more than fine. By the time Usain passed the baton to Asafa, Jamaica led by three metres. The gap only got wider as Asafa flew down the track. They won by almost one whole second, an even bigger margin than Usain's two previous races.

Usain was a triple Olympic champion. He had won three golds in six days. Not only that, he had broken three world records too.

'I'm going to need an extra luggage allowance for all these medals,' he joked to Coach Mills as they headed to the airport after the Olympics were over.

His coach smiled. There would be new challenges to come and new rivals to beat, but for now Usain could relax and enjoy what had been the most unbelievable experience of his life.

CHAPTER 14

THE BEST GETS BETTER

'How do you top that?'

That was the question everyone was asking Usain in the months that followed his outstanding performances in Beijing. His mom, his pops, NJ, old friends from Coxheath, people on the streets of Kingston – they all asked him the same thing.

In Usain's mind, perhaps there was no way to top it. His world had exploded since returning home from China. From the moment his plane touched down at Kingston airport, he was mobbed by fans – and that continued everywhere he went. He met many famous people, from the Jamaican Prime Minister to the Chelsea footballer Didier Drogba, whom he met on a trip to London.

'I just want to say how much I loved watching you race in Beijing,' Didier said.

Usain was speechless. This was the wrong way round – it was he who loved watching Didier play week-in week-out for Chelsea!

As always, it was Coach Mills who had the answer for what would come next.

'You need to work even harder, Bolt.'

Usain groaned. Hadn't he been working hard enough?

'You are the number one sprinter in the world and everyone wants to beat you. The 100m sprinters and the 200m sprinters – they're all out to get you. The World Championships in Berlin are coming up. If you want to top Beijing, do it all again in Berlin. You need to run even faster to prove that Beijing was no flash in the pan.'

Flash in the pan? Usain couldn't believe what he was hearing. He boiled with anger inside. But his coach's words had exactly the right effect, as they made Usain determined to destroy his competitors again.

In early 2009, though, his preparations suffered a serious setback when he was involved in a car crash just outside Kingston. Luckily, he managed to escape with only some injuries to his feet, but he would still have to miss several weeks of training. Coach Mills was just relieved that he was okay.

'Some things in life are more important than major championships, Bolt,' he said. 'But don't worry, we'll get you ready for Berlin in time.'

By the time the 100m final in Berlin arrived, Usain was more than ready. He had lived the life of a monk for the previous six weeks, dedicating himself to training, going to bed early instead of partying, and avoiding any bad food – even his favourite chicken nuggets.

Usain was in playful mood as he lined up for the start of the race. He bounced around, laughing for the cameras. When he shot his Lightning Bolt, the Olympiastadion went ballistic.

The sense of playfulness was infectious. Daniel Bailey – Usain's friend who was also trained by Coach Mills – pretended to write his name on the

TV camera lens. When the camera came to Asafa Powell, he fooled around too, putting his race number over his mouth. The crowd was loving it.

Tyson Gay was in no mood to mess around, though. Usain's American rival was back and meant business, desperate to make up for missing out in Beijing. His face was a picture of concentration.

When the fun was over, Usain settled on his blocks and waited for the gun. This was his chance to prove he was the real deal, more than just a flash in the pan.

Bang!

With those thoughts flying through his mind, he tore down the bright blue track of the Olympiastadion. Nobody could keep up with him, not even Tyson.

The clock stopped at 9.58 seconds. Usain had done the unthinkable. He had run even faster than in Beijing.

He screamed with joy. The crowd screamed even louder. He stretched his arms out like an aeroplane as he jogged around the stadium, lapping up the applause. The Olympic champion was now the world champion.

'Was that quick enough for you, Coach?' Usain teased Coach Mills after the race.

'Don't get too confident, Bolt. You've still got the 200m and the relay to come. And people will want to beat you *even* more now.'

But in reality, Usain's confidence couldn't get any higher. He knew at that moment in time that he was the fastest man in the world, without question; if he performed to the best of his ability, no one could beat him. It was the same thought he'd had all those years ago at Waldensia Primary after finally getting the better of his nemesis Ricardo.

Competing in major championships brought the best out of him. The thrill of competition and the roar of the crowd only made him run faster. He loved delivering performances that the fans would never forget.

And that's exactly what he did in the 200m final, tearing around the track in yet another world record of 19.19 seconds. Once again, the fans went mad for their hero.

Usain was absolutely exhausted after his exploits in the 100m and 200m, but nothing could stop him from lining up in the relay. The Jamaican quartet was slightly different from the one at the Olympics, with Steve Mullings replacing Nesta Carter, but the result was exactly the same. Asafa romped home to seal another gold, and a third world title for Usain.

There was no world record this time, but Usain didn't care. He had done exactly what Coach Mills had asked of him and had somehow managed to top his individual world records from Beijing. With victory in the relay, he now had a lovely set of three world gold medals to go alongside his Olympic collection – two days after turning twenty-three. It was the perfect belated birthday present.

CHAPTER 15

A FALSE DAWN

'Hey coach, who's that kid on the track?' Usain asked. 'He's running some pretty speedy times.'

'That's Yohan Blake, Bolt. And if you're not careful, he'll be overtaking you soon.'

Usain smiled. He knew Coach Mills well enough by now to understand that he was trying to motivate him. 'We'll see about that,' he thought.

Truth be told, Usain had first spotted Yohan a while ago and had been keeping an eye on him ever since. He was three years younger than Usain and six inches shorter, but his whole body bulged with muscle. What Usain really noticed was how hard he tried in training. Every time Usain did a sprint alongside Yohan, the younger Jamaican tried everything he could to win.

'Yo, Blake, you don't need to win every time on the training track,' Usain said one day as the sprinter blazed off into the distance. 'Save yourself for the big races that really matter.'

But the next session was exactly the same. Yohan had to cross the line first.

Usain laughed, shaking his head. 'What's wrong with you, bro? You're a beast.'

And so a nickname was born. From then on, Yohan was known as 'The Beast'.

Usain regularly handed out advice to the other athletes at the Racers Track Club. He wanted to help them develop by sharing as much as knowledge as he could from what he'd learned as an athlete and competing at the championships. He would chat about everything from running techniques and preparation to handling the pressure of the big occasion. Usain believed that anything he could say to help his fellow sprinters improve could only be a good thing. And if one day, they improved so much that they became his rival, then he would have to deal with them on the track.

With no major championships on the schedule
for 2010, Usain had agreed with Coach Mills that
he would have a lighter training programme that
season to let his body recover. He split most of his
time between hanging out at his new home, where
he lived with his half-brother Sadiki and NJ, and the
training track – plus going partying from time to time
in Kingston.

While there were no gold medals up for grabs,
Usain still entered lots of races. He had become an
international superstar, and fans all around the world
filled stadiums to see him race. At the end of the
day, running had always been fun for Usain, and he
wanted to pass the fun onto the fans. He travelled
to all parts of the world to race – Brazil, England,
China, Italy – and no one went home until they had
seen the Lightning Bolt pose.

Usain enjoyed putting on a show for the
spectators, but what really motivated him was
winning the major races, and as 2011 dawned, he
had his eyes firmly set on the World Championships.

There was something bothering him, however. He

couldn't get his start of the race right and was often slow out of the blocks. Even when he started well in training, he would slip up in the races themselves. That meant he had to work harder to catch the other runners, especially in the shorter distance of the 100m.

Coach Mills was worried too.

'Relax, Bolt. You've proved you can deliver on the world stage. It will be fine when you're out there,' he said when they arrived in Daegu in South Korea for the World Championships.

Usain knew what his coach said made sense. He was the strong favourite for the 100m gold, particularly as several leading contenders were absent. The main threat would come from his training partner, Yohan. The pair had become good friends back in Kingston, but any friendships went out of the window now there was a world title at stake.

Usain was determined to defend his title from Berlin, even more so as his parents would be watching in the crowd, but he still couldn't stop thinking about his starts. It didn't help that there had recently been a rule change in the sport. In years gone by, athletes had been allowed to make one false start and were only disqualified from a race if they did it twice. Now, anyone who false-started once would be disqualified immediately. No second chances.

Usain tried to forget all about it as he lined up for the 100m final, but he couldn't relax and fool about like usual. 'What if I mess up my start again?' he said to himself. 'I've got to get this right.'

The Daegu crowd fell silent as the runners settled in their blocks, waiting for the starter's orders.

'Must get a good start,' Usain whispered to himself. He rose in the blocks. Another gold medal was less than ten seconds away, if he could just take his chance.

He wanted to win.

Right now.

Usain left the blocks a split second before the gun fired. He knew instantly he had gone too early. The gun fired again, signalling that there had been a false start.

The entire stadium gasped. Surely not?

The reigning champion had false-started.

Usain was out.

He couldn't believe what he had done. As he jogged down the track, he pulled his vest over his head, then ripped it off completely. He was so angry with himself. He knew it was his fault. There was no one else to blame.

He had to leave the track but stayed in the stadium to watch Yohan take the gold. The winning time was 9.92 seconds – a lot slower than Usain usually ran – but he was happy for his teammate and congratulated him. It was the right thing to do.

When he spoke to his parents the next day, Usain was still furious. He felt bad that they had flown all that way and he hadn't even completed the race.

'Forget about it, son,' Wellesley said. 'These things happen in sport. You're lucky that you have two more chances to win gold this week.'

'Remember what you always say, VJ – running should be fun,' his mom added. 'Go out there and have a good time.'

It was great advice. Usain realised he had been worrying too much and he needed to have fun again, so that the good results would then return.

He was in a far more positive mood when he returned to the track for the 200m final and, after the start was safely negotiated, he breezed to victory.

'Phew!' he said as he crossed the line. It felt amazing to be on top of the podium again.

The following evening, he was back on the podium once more, this time with his Jamaican teammates after they broke their own world record in the relay.

'What a difference a few days make,' Usain said to his parents as he hugged them after the race. The false start was already a fading memory and Usain knew he would never make the same mistake again.

CHAPTER 16

FIGHTING TALK

'Yo, VJ, did you hear what Justin Gatlin's been saying about you?' NJ asked.

There was no response. Usain was sitting on the sofa, watching his favourite football team, Manchester United, play on TV. He didn't like being disturbed when United were on.

NJ continued. 'He's been talking himself up. He says that he already has one Olympic gold medal and he's going to the London Olympics to win another one.'

Usain raised an eyebrow but didn't shift his gaze from the TV screen.

'And then he said: "Everyone has watched the Bolt show for a couple of years and now everyone wants to see someone else in the mix – hopefully I can take charge of that".'

Usain spun around instantly. 'He said what?'

NJ started laughing. He knew that would get his attention!

Usain couldn't believe it. Gatlin had returned to professional athletics after his ban and was running some good times again. His comments had come after he had beaten Asafa Powell over 100m, a result he had celebrated by walking down the track firing imaginary gunshots.

'He's acting like he's won Olympic gold, not some race in Qatar,' Usain thought.

The next day at training, Coach Mills offered some valuable advice.

'What do you expect, Bolt? For four years, you've been the number one man. It's Olympic year and all the best sprinters are coming after you. Justin Gatlin wants to get a reaction out of you by saying these things – my advice is to ignore it.'

Usain nodded. 'Sure. I prefer to let my running do the talking, Coach.'

Usain was wise enough not to let a few taunting words bother him too much, but his conversation with Coach Mills had raised a good point – with the London Olympics only a few months away, all his main rivals were hungry for gold and hitting top form.

Gatlin added a victory in the USA to his Qatar win. Tyson Gay bagged a couple of big wins in Paris and London. Asafa was on fire in Shanghai. Usain had not been happy with his own form in 2012, though, and these results served as a reminder that he couldn't afford to take his foot off the gas.

The person whom many experts thought would be his biggest threat was right under his nose at the Racers Track Club. Yohan Blake had grown in confidence since making the most of Usain's false start in Daegu to become world champion. In June 2012, The Beast served further notice of his strong form when he beat a classy field in New York over 100m. A few weeks later, Usain came face to face with his training partner at the Jamaican Olympic trials.

With only three spots available on the Jamaican

team for both the 100m and 200m, competition for places was extremely tough. As well as Yohan, Usain was up against Asafa and two fellow relay gold medallists in Michael Frater and Nesta Carter.

'Man, this is a harder race than the Olympic final,' Usain said to himself as he looked down the line before the start of the 100m at the Kingston National Stadium.

Unfortunately for Usain, he failed to reproduce the form that saw him win the world junior title in the same stadium all those years ago. A poor start left him in last spot, as Yohan sprinted into the distance.

'Just make sure you get in the top three,' he thought as he clawed back the gap to the other competitors. 'There's no way you're missing London.'

He did just enough to finish second ahead of Asafa but couldn't catch Yohan, who set a new personal best time of 9.75.

The next day brought a new event – the 200m – but exactly the same result. Yohan first, Usain second.

Although he had qualified for the Olympics, Usain

was far from happy. The 200m was *his* event. He was hardly ever beaten. He wasn't used to losing. It was a new feeling and he didn't like it. Making the loss even harder to stomach was Yohan's reaction as he crossed the line, putting a finger to his mouth as if he was telling everyone to 'ssshhhhh'. Usain never liked being told to keep quiet.

He walked away from the track that night with a lot on his mind. On the one hand, he had qualified for the Olympics, but losing twice to Yohan in as many days was a bitter pill to swallow. Yet, in a funny way, it had helped him. He realised he would have to improve significantly and work harder than ever in training if he was to successfully defend his Olympic titles.

Four years earlier, he had written his name into Olympic history by winning three golds. If he could repeat the feat, he would become an Olympic great. The London Olympics would be even bigger than Beijing and Usain was up for the challenge.

CHAPTER 17

LONDON (PART 1)

From the moment his plane landed in London, Usain knew the 2012 Olympics were going to be the biggest, craziest two weeks of his life.

The city had gone Olympic mad. Everything was about the Games, from all the shops inside the airport selling merchandise to the advertising billboards on the side of the road. Even the famous Tower Bridge over the River Thames had the Olympic rings hanging down from it.

For one of the rare moments in his life, Usain was stunned into silence, and he got an even bigger shock when he looked out of the bus window to see an enormous picture of himself grinning back at him. As one of the big stars of the Olympics, his image had been used on numerous posters and billboards throughout London.

'I'm getting sick of the sight of you and we've only just got here,' said Asafa with a cheeky grin.

'You'll be even more sick when you see me racing off into the distance to win the 100m,' Usain laughed.

It wasn't just London that was getting excited about seeing Usain in action. When he arrived in the Olympic Village, he was bombarded by other athletes. Every time he stepped out of the Jamaican apartment block, he was greeted by people wanting to shake his hand, take a photo or wish him luck.

It was bedlam. Even the short walk to the dining hall could take up to fifteen minutes. On the plus side, when he reached the hall, there was a much greater choice of food than in Beijing, so he didn't have to eat chicken nuggets every meal – although he still consumed a few.

Usain had a big job to do on the very first night of the Games. He was chosen to be Jamaica's flag-bearer at the Opening Ceremony, which meant he would lead the Jamaican team around the Olympic Stadium in the athletes' parade.

'Don't drop the flag, Usain. There are only a few hundred million people watching you on TV right now,' Yohan Blake teased his teammate as they walked into the stadium.

'More like a billion,' added Asafa, giving Usain a friendly nudge.

Usain smiled. He didn't care. It was an enormous honour to carry the flag of his country and he waved it with pride. As he looked around the Olympic Stadium, packed to the rafters with 80,000 people, all on their feet and cheering, he could only imagine what the atmosphere would be like for the 100m final.

A week later, when he returned to the Olympic Stadium for his first heat, there wasn't a spare seat in the house.

'What's going on, Coach? The morning athletics sessions are usually half-empty at the Olympics or World Championships.'

'Not in London, Bolt. The people here are sports-mad. The tickets sold out months ago.'

Usain was delighted to see that there were lots of fans wearing yellow, green and black in the crowd. London had a big Jamaican population and he received a tremendous reception when he walked onto the track – it felt like a second home.

In fact, the whole stadium, not just the Jamaicans, erupted when Usain appeared.

'Usain, Usain, Usain!'

Usain responded with a wave and a little dance in the morning sun.

After he won his heat, the fanfare continued.

'We love Bolt! We love Bolt!'

Come the following evening, Usain couldn't wait to get back into the Olympic Stadium for the final. Twenty-four hours earlier, he had watched spellbound on TV as Great Britain won three Olympic gold medals – Jessica Ennis in the heptathlon, Greg Rutherford in the long jump and the brilliant long-distance runner Mo Farah in the 10,000m. The day was being called 'Super Saturday' and the fans in the stadium had gone mad.

Usain was hoping for a similar reaction in his final.

He knew he would need to be at his best if he was to defend his Olympic title. All the big names had qualified for the final – Asafa and Yohan, as well as the two Americans, Tyson Gay and his big rival, Justin Gatlin, who had been talking himself up in the build-up to the Games.

'You can talk the talk, but let's see if you can walk the walk,' Usain thought as he waited at the start line.

The atmosphere was electric, but so noisy that the finalists had to wait longer than usual at the start; Usain even jokingly put his finger to his lips to help everyone quieten down.

Finally, the gun sounded. As the eight finalists stormed out of the blocks, there was a fireworks show of flashbulbs and bright lights from all the cameras and fans' phones. Then there came the roar of the crowd. The loudest roar Usain had ever heard.

Gatlin began like a bullet. Usain, meanwhile, was slow out of the blocks after taking care not to false-start. He could see that Asafa was already out of contention after injuring his leg, but his other rivals were flying. He dug deep.

By the halfway mark Usain was back on level terms. It didn't seem possible to him, but the cheering from the fans became even louder. It spurred him on. By the sixty-metre mark, he was in front of Yohan, with Gatlin back in third. He was getting faster and faster.

Unlike in Beijing, he didn't start celebrating until he crossed the line, stopping the clock at 9.63 seconds – the fastest ever 100m run at the Olympics. Yohan finished second in 9.75, his victory at the trials already a distant memory. Taking bronze was Gatlin in 9.79 – when it came to the crunch, he was no match for the champion.

Usain had won a fourth Olympic gold medal.

Cue some crazy celebrations. With Yohan at his side, Usain fooled around with the fans on his lap of honour, pulling out some dance moves and even doing a forward roll on the track.

'You should be in the gymnastics competition, not athletics,' Yohan laughed.

It was the perfect start to Usain's Olympic campaign. He was one step closer to achieving his dream of successfully defending all three Olympic titles from Beijing. No one in the history of the Olympics had ever done that before.

One down, two to go.

CHAPTER 18

LONDON (PART 2)

Grant true wisdom from above
Justice, truth be ours forever
Jamaica, land we love
Jamaica, Jamaica, Jamaica, land we love.

Usain welled up with pride as he sang the last lines of the Jamaican national anthem. He was back in the Olympic Stadium twenty-four hours after winning the 100m final, this time to receive his gold medal. It was such a special feeling to stand on top of the podium. He knew all the people back home would be watching.

When the anthem finished, the crowd burst into rapturous applause. Usain smiled, waved and wagged his finger – just as he had done when he

crossed the finish line. As he made his way out of
the stadium with the two other medallists, Yohan
Blake and Justin Gatlin, he mouthed to the fans:
'See you tomorrow.' He would soon be back in the
Olympic Stadium to begin part two of his London
mission: the 200m.

The next morning, Usain was in a mischievous
mood. With the start of his heat only minutes away,
he had a chat with the volunteer standing in his lane,
a sixteen-year-old called George whose job was to
look after the box containing Usain's clothes.

'What's up, George? Are you enjoying yourself?'
Usain asked, giving George a friendly fist-pump.

'I'm loving it, Usain.'

He noticed that George kept looking at the woolly
hat in his box. Even though it was summer in
England, to a Jamaican like Usain it felt pretty cold
first thing in the morning and so he wrapped up
warm before the race.

'Here you go, George. Have a souvenir,' he said,
chucking his hat to his new friend, just as the
starter called the runners to their blocks. The crowd

roared their approval as George's face lit up with glee.

Usain breezed through his heat in first place. It was exactly the same story the next day in the semi-finals as he comfortably booked his place in the final.

With the 100m title already in the bag, Usain was full of confidence and ready to set the record straight with Yohan after his defeat in the trials. They were joined in the final by another countryman – Warren Weir – who also had hopes of winning a medal. It was yet another sign of the strength of Jamaican sprinting in London. Barely did a day pass without a Jamaican athlete winning another Olympic medal. Like Usain, Shelly-Ann Fraser-Pryce retained her 100m title from Beijing, with teammate Veronica Campbell-Brown taking bronze, and then Shelly-Ann also won silver in the 200m. Hansle Parchment added another bronze in the men's 110m hurdles.

Usain enjoyed watching his teammates win medals almost as much as winning them himself. He was so proud that his Caribbean island of less than three million people could compete with, and often beat, the giants of the athletics world like the USA and Russia.

Right now, though, as the seconds ticked down to the start of the 200m final, he focused on beating his training partner from back in Kingston. Usain had remained undefeated in the 200m at all major championships since Beijing. He had no intention of that record changing any time soon.

Once again, while the other finalists were firmly focused on the race ahead, Usain joked around with the volunteers, asking one girl if she wanted to run the race for him.

In truth, while it looked to the watching world as if he didn't care, Usain used his pre-race antics – chatting with volunteers, bouncing around, dancing – to block out any nerves. It also made time fly by, as before he knew it, he was on his blocks and the starter's gun fired.

They were off!

'The fans have been so amazing. Let's see if they can cheer even louder tonight,' Usain thought as he shot into the lead.

Three lanes separated Usain from Yohan and, although he couldn't see him around the bend, he knew his training partner well enough to be certain he would be close by. Sure enough, as they hit the straight, he caught a glimpse of Yohan out of the corner of his eye.

'Not today, Beast,' Usain thought as he stretched out and surged ahead once more.

As he approached the finish line, he could even afford to slow down slightly. He looked across at Yohan and put his fingers to his lips, mimicking the 'ssshhhhhh' gesture of his teammate a couple of months earlier. Usain had made his point – the 200m was his event. He still couldn't silence the cheers of the crowd, though.

Usain ran a lightning-quick time of 19.32, which could have been even faster if he hadn't slowed before the line. Yohan took his second silver medal of the Games, while Warren made it a Jamaican hat-trick of medals.

It was an extraordinary performance by Usain. No man in the history of the Olympics had ever

defended both the 100m and 200m titles before –
and he was in the mood to party.

First of all, he got down on the track and did
five press-ups: one for each of his Olympic gold
medals. Then he borrowed a camera from one of
the trackside photographers and started taking
some snaps of his own – of the fans, Yohan and
even himself!

Last but not least was the tradition of the Lightning
Bolt. The move was so popular now that everyone in
London seemed to be doing it, and on this occasion
even the Olympic mascot Wenlock joined in.

'I'm now a living legend,' Usain said in his post-
race interview. 'Now I am going to sit back, relax
and think about what's next.'

'What about the relay?' the interviewer whispered.

Usain laughed. 'Oh yeah. How could I forget?
Don't tell my coach I said that. Don't worry, I'll be
ready for it.'

The podium for the next day's medal ceremony
had a distinctly Jamaican feel. Usain was on the top
step where he belonged, with Yohan and Warren

on either side. All three of the medallists knew the words of the anthem off by heart.

Grant true wisdom from above
Justice, truth be ours forever
Jamaica, land we love
Jamaica, Jamaica, Jamaica, land we love.

CHAPTER 19

LONDON (PART 3)

'Okay boys, listen up,' Usain shouted, beckoning his teammates to come into a huddle.

The four Jamaican athletes – Nesta Carter, Michael Frater, Yohan Blake and Usain – stood in a circle with their arms around each other.

'Tonight's relay is the final athletics race of the whole Olympics. We have been running really well in practice – if everything goes well, we could break the world record.'

It was a magical thought. Usain had already won two gold medals and now had a great chance of winning a third in the 4x100m relay – just like he'd done in Beijing. It would be the icing on the cake if he could finish with a world record.

'I can't believe the Games are almost over,' Yohan said as they did some final stretches.

'I know, all the more reason to bring the curtain down on the Olympics in style,' Usain replied with a grin.

Although there was a lot of pressure on Usain in his bid to become the first ever athlete to win three sprinting golds at successive Games, he didn't show any sign of nerves. He enjoyed running the relay with his friends. Unlike in the individual races, there was no rivalry with Yohan, Nesta or Michael as they were all on the same team. And Usain had loved being part of a team ever since the days when he first played cricket.

There was also plenty of joking going on. Usain ran the fourth and final leg of the relay, meaning he would receive the baton from Yohan.

'Come on, Beast, I haven't got all day. What's taking you so long?' Usain teased his teammate in training as he waited for the baton.

Yohan smiled. 'If you just let me run the final leg, then we wouldn't have this problem.'

It was a big honour to run the last leg and bring the team home to the finish line. Usain laughed before giving a two-word reply.

'No chance!'

He knew that the very fact they were practising baton handovers spelt bad news for their rivals. Usain couldn't remember doing that at any previous championships; usually they just turned up and relied on their speed to get them around the track, not any quick changeovers. Now, with four rapid runners plus lightning-quick handovers, they really meant business.

Jamaica had drawn lane 6 for the final. Their biggest rivals, the USA, were right beside them in lane 7. With Justin Gatlin, Tyson Gay and another finalist from the 100m, Ryan Bailey, the Americans would be tough to beat, but Usain wasn't concerned. He had complete faith in his team.

As he waited for the race to start, Usain kept the crowd entertained, pulling the Lightning Bolt pose and flexing his muscles like a bodybuilder. The gun sounded and Nesta burst out of the blocks. All the practice paid off as his teammates swiftly transferred the baton around the track. Gatlin ran a storming second leg for the USA, but Yohan's third leg was even better, giving Usain a slight lead when he took the baton.

For one last time, the London crowd rose to their feet and roared him to the finish. Usain responded in the only way he knew how – by running even faster.

And this time, unlike in the 200m a couple of nights earlier or the 100m in Beijing, he didn't slow down at the end, even though victory was guaranteed. Lunging for the line, he stopped the clock at 36.84 seconds. No team had ever run under 37 seconds before in the history of the sport.

It was a new world record!

After winning the 100m, Usain had performed a forward roll. After winning the 200m, he had done press-ups. This time, he wanted to do something different entirely and pay tribute to the athletics hero of the home fans: Mo Farah. Earlier that night, the British runner had won the 5,000m, adding another gold medal to his 10,000m title a week earlier. Like

Usain, Mo had his own special celebration, putting both hands on top of his head in the shape of the letter M. It was known as the 'Mo-bot'.

So what did Usain decide to do when he crossed the line? His own Mo-bot pose of course!

The fans loved that celebration, and Usain and the rest of the team got an incredible reception in the Olympic Stadium on their lap of honour.

The only strange moment came when an official tried to take the baton off Usain after the race.

'Can I have the baton back, Mr Bolt?'

'I'd like to keep it as a souvenir please,' Usain replied.

'Sorry, the rules are the rules.'

Usain shrugged his shoulders and handed it over. There was no point arguing. Suddenly, the stadium erupted into boos – the fans had been watching the whole incident. Luckily, common sense soon prevailed and Usain was allowed to keep the baton. It was another win to go with his three golds.

The 4x100m relay gold medal was Jamaica's fourth of the Olympic Games. It took the country's overall medal tally to twelve – four golds, four silvers and four bronzes – after the women's relay teams had both finished on the podium. It was the most medals ever won by Jamaica at the Olympics, and all of them had come in athletics.

That achievement made Usain and his teammates even prouder as they stood on the podium to collect their medals.

After the ceremony, as the medallists started walking off the track for the last time, Usain felt a range of emotions. He was over the moon to have won three gold medals again, but he was sad that the most incredible Olympic experience was coming to an end. As he waved goodbye to the crowd, he heard a chant going around the stadium.

'What are they singing?' he wondered.

It grew louder and louder and louder until there was no mistaking it.

We want Bolt!

We want Bolt!

We want Bolt!

Seizing his opportunity, Usain snuck away from

the official photo with his teammates and the other
medallists from the USA and Trinidad and Tobago.
He turned to the crowd and started pumping his fist
in time to their chanting.

We want Bolt!

We want Bolt!

We want Bolt!

Always the showman, Usain paused for a
moment. Everyone in the stadium knew what was
coming next.

He drew back his arms, pointed up and fired his
Lightning Bolt into the sky. The crowd let out the
loudest cheer of the whole Olympics.

CHAPTER 20

SINGING IN THE RAIN

As the 2013 season arrived, Usain was struggling for motivation. The London Olympics had been simply the most incredible experience. He had already achieved more in athletics, and won more medals, than he had ever believed possible. The World Championships in Russia were on the horizon, with the chance for yet more glory, but the thought of all the work he would need to do to hit peak form didn't excite him.

Competing in the big events was what gave Usain a real buzz – while he understood the importance of training, it had never been his favourite pastime.

On the plus side, some of the hard work had been done for him before he even needed to think about training. Three of his big rivals would be missing from the World Championships – Yohan Blake was injured, and neither Tyson Gay nor Asafa Powell was competing in 2013.

'Maybe I could just take it easy in training for a few months,' he thought.

There was no escaping the threat of Justin Gatlin, though. He might have been four years older than Usain, but the American seemed to be improving with age. After winning a 100m bronze in London, he had begun the new season with a bang, claiming victories in his first two races.

Nevertheless, Usain was confident he still had the measure of his rival – and that certainly seemed to be the case at the start of their 100m race in Rome when the pair came face to face for the first time in 2013.

As Usain sprang out of the blocks and took an early lead, he seemed set for yet another win over the American. However, something unexpected started to happen: Gatlin fought back. He drew level with Usain. As Usain's legs began to tire, the

American moved ahead. Usain strained to close the gap, throwing his head forward at the finish, but it was not quite enough. Gatlin won by 0.01 seconds – a tiny margin, but a victory nonetheless.

The Rome crowd gasped. It was very rare for Usain to be beaten, and even more unusual for him to be overtaken when he had been leading.

After the race, a pumped-up Gatlin had a message for the world – he was coming to get Usain.

'I had a different feeling going into this season than I did last year,' he said. 'I train to be number one – that's what I'm shooting for.'

Usain listened with interest. He wasn't in top shape yet so wasn't too worried about the result, but he never liked losing. And he especially didn't like hearing that his status as the world's top sprinter could be under threat.

He decided to keep these thoughts to himself for now. 'At least I ran under ten seconds!' he joked with the interviewer in Rome.

But it was no laughing matter when he got back to Coach Mills at the Racers Track Club in Kingston.

'You need to get into shape, Bolt – and fast – unless you want to watch Gatlin jumping around in Moscow with your 100m gold medal around his neck. No more taking it easy.'

One of the great things about Coach Mills was he had a knack of inspiring Usain to produce amazing performances.

'Listen, Bolt, you're still a young man – only twenty-six years old. Do you know how old the great American sprinter Carl Lewis was when he won his last Olympic gold medal?'

Usain stared blankly at his coach. He had never been very good at studying athletics history.

'Thirty-five,' he continued, 'so you've got plenty more years left at the top. And if you win three gold medals in Moscow, you'll have eight world titles. Do you know who else has won eight world titles?'

Again, Usain was at a loss. He hated history tests!

'Michael Johnson, that's who.'

This time, the answer made him take notice. To equal the record of his hero Michael Johnson – now that would be cool.

'Right, best get to work then,' Coach Mills said, seeing a spark of interest light up Usain's face.

Come Moscow, after an intense training campaign, Usain was fighting fit and ready to defend his status as the world's leading sprinter. The pain from false-starting at the World Championships two years earlier still lingered. He was hungry to be on top of the podium once again.

If he was going to win, not only would he have to defeat Gatlin, but also deal with the Moscow weather. An almighty thunderstorm arrived just before the 100m final. It poured with rain.

Usain took it all in his stride. 'I thought this was an athletics race, not a swimming final,' he joked with his teammate Nesta Carter as they splashed their way to the starting blocks. The conditions were terrible for sprinting but Usain wasn't too concerned – he realised all the finalists faced the same problems.

Gatlin was buzzing with adrenaline before the start. He paced up and down in his lane like a lion stalking his prey, shouting, 'Let's go, let's go' into the TV camera.

Right beside Gatlin, in lane 6, Usain was altogether calmer. When the camera focused on him, he opened an imaginary umbrella to protect himself from the rain. The entire Luzhniki Stadium howled with laughter.

As the gun sounded, the roles from Rome were reversed. This time, it was Gatlin who made the better start and left Usain trailing.

But Usain didn't panic or strain to catch up. He knew he had done all the training and was confident in his own ability. With each massive stride, he got ever closer to Gatlin, and then got ever further ahead. He crossed the line first in 9.77 seconds – not a world record, but an unbelievable time considering he was running through puddles.

As he started to slow down, a massive bolt of lightning lit up the sky. Even the weather was doing the Lightning Bolt pose.

Usain had proved yet again that he was the undisputed world number one, and in the days that followed he cemented that reputation, winning both the 200m and the relay. Sprinting past his rival Gatlin on the last leg of the relay to claim gold for Jamaica was the icing on the cake. To show his appreciation for the crowd's support, Usain had prepared a special celebration. He took off his running shoes, crouched down with his arms folded – and kicked out his legs in a special Russian dance. All performed at Lightning Bolt speed.

CHAPTER 21

GOOD VERSUS EVIL

'On your marks.'

After months of talking and months of speculation, it now all came down to the next ten seconds – or slightly less. It was the race everyone – athletics fans, sports fans and anyone who was near a TV – wanted to see. Usain Bolt v Justin Gatlin in the 2015 World Championships.

Two years had passed since Usain had last raced against his American rival in Moscow, and the tables had turned in that time. Usain had been plagued by injuries. He had missed large chunks of the 2014 season, a rare highlight coming at the Commonwealth Games in Glasgow when he anchored the Jamaican relay team to victory. In typical fashion, he delighted the Scottish fans with his post-race celebrations, posing for selfies in a tartan hat.

For most of the year, however, he had been forced to sit back and watch as Gatlin dominated the 100m all around the world, posting seven of the ten quickest times all season. Usain didn't enjoy that. He wasn't a good armchair viewer – unless he was watching the West Indies play cricket or Manchester United in the Premier League.

'Set.'

Things went from bad to worse for Usain in 2015 as he continued to struggle with injuries. It was so frustrating for him not to be able to compete and it didn't help that Gatlin was thriving in his absence. As the Bejing World Championships approached, the American was unbeatable, running the four fastest times of any sprinter in the world – 9.74, 9.75 twice, and 9.78. Coming into the final, he had won 28 races in a row.

Usain, on the other hand, had only managed to run three 100m races all season, and his best time wasn't close to his rival's. All of which meant that lots of people were predicting that Usain's reign as the best sprinter in the world might be nearing an end.

'Don't write me off,' Usain thought. He wasn't ready to give up his title just yet.

Bang.

They were off. Crucially, Usain didn't repeat his mistake from a couple of hours earlier. At the start of his semi-final, he had tripped out of the blocks and had to use all his strength not to fall over. For a fleeting moment, he feared he might not even make it to the final, but he surged from the back of the field to sneak first place on the line in a desperately close finish with three other athletes. His time of 9.96 seconds was much slower than Gatlin's, who eased to victory in 9.77.

Even so, Usain wasn't too concerned. 'Let's see how he deals with the pressure of being the favourite in the final,' he thought.

'Bolt gets out pretty well. Gatlin's got out a little better though.'

Advantage Gatlin. In the first thirty metres of

the final, the American held a slender lead. Usain could see the red shirt of his rival out of the corner of his eye, two lanes away from him. Gatlin was a better starter, but as long as Usain could stay within touching distance, he would have a chance. He always improved the longer the race went on – and he knew that thought would be at the back of his rival's mind too.

'Bolt and Gatlin are right together.'

By the halfway point, there was nothing to choose between them. Spurred on by the cheers of the fans in the Bird's Nest, Usain had clawed back the advantage. This was the track where seven years earlier he had made headlines around the world by winning three Olympic golds. He had a special relationship with the Beijing fans and he could feel that they were on his side once again.

In fact, most sports fans on the planet were on Usain's side. The race had been billed as good versus evil – Usain, the champion and superhero of athletics, against Gatlin, the challenger who had returned to athletics after being banned for cheating.

While Usain enjoyed the support, what he really cared about was beating his rival, retaining his title and giving the Beijing fans another golden moment.

'Here is Gatlin taking the lead.'

But retaining his title would be easier said than done. It was now a two-horse race, and as the pair moved clear of the rest of the field with forty metres remaining, it was Gatlin who hit the front again. He was showing all the strength and speed that had helped him win those twenty-eight races.

Yet Usain was not prepared to give up without a fight. He had been the king of the sport for the past seven years. Championships brought the best out of him. He was certain Gatlin would be wondering why he wasn't further ahead.

'Keep putting the pressure on,' Usain thought.

'But here comes Usain Bolt.'

With thirty metres remaining, the pressure started to show. Gatlin's running technique – normally so smooth – completely fell apart. He started stumbling, arms and legs flailing in the air.

Usain seized upon the mistake. Arms pumping,

knees flying high in the air, he motored to the finish. In the final metres, he threw his head forward to cross the line. Gatlin did exactly the same. It was incredibly close – so close that even the commentator wasn't sure who had won.

'And Bolt gets it, or does he? It's very, very tight but I think he's done it.'

Usain thought he'd done it too, but he wasn't going to pull out the Lightning Bolt victory pose just yet. In most of his races in years gone by, he was so far ahead that as soon as he crossed the line he could start celebrating – or even before. But this time he chose to wait for the result of the photo finish.

The next 25 seconds seemed like 25 minutes for Usain, but at long last an enormous roar from the crowd told him everything he needed to know, as the result flashed up on the big screen:

Usain Bolt 9.79

Usain was the 100m world champion again. He had won by just 0.01 seconds, the exact same time difference as when Gatlin had beaten him in Rome. Except this time, Usain was the winner.

The two rivals hugged after the result was announced. Usain had always believed it was important to show good sportsmanship – regardless of the result.

Once again, he had proven that when it came to the major races, whatever the circumstances or whatever had happened previously, he was the man to beat.

It was Usain's ninth world title, and the sweetest of them all.

CHAPTER 22

WILL HE OR WON'T HE?

It was a moment that sent shockwaves around the sporting world. Newspapers all over the globe, from America to Australia, shouted out the story on their front pages.

Olympic legend in injury scare!

Usain could miss Rio de Janeiro Olympics!

Bolt in race against time to make Games!

Usain was injured. With only one month to go until the Rio Olympics of 2016, the defending champion – who was bidding to win three gold medals for the third Games in a row – was in danger of missing the world's biggest sporting party.

He had been competing in the Jamaican trials for the Olympics when he hurt his thigh. The injury was so bad that he sat out the final. Luckily, the Jamaican selectors decided that Usain would be given a 'medical exemption', which meant he could have a place on the Olympic team, but only if he was fit enough.

As the world collectively held its breath, Usain himself was far more chilled out – as was so often the case. The injury didn't feel too painful and the main reason he had chosen to miss the final was to avoid the risk of making it any worse.

'When I was younger, I probably would have insisted on running that race,' he said to Coach Mills.

'But over the years, I've learned how to manage my body… with your help, of course,' he added with a laugh.

Throughout his career, Usain had faced many obstacles – all the injury problems as a teenager, recovering from a car crash, the false start in the world 100m final, getting the better of his rival Justin Gatlin. Each time, he had overcome the challenge.

Now, though, he faced another problem and he

knew exactly what he needed to do. 'It's time to pay another visit to the doctor.'

If there was one man who could save his Olympic dream, it was Dr Hans-Wilhelm Müller-Wohlfahrt. Based in Germany, the doctor was one of the world's leading experts on treating sports injuries. Usain had first flown to see him when he was suffering with back and leg problems as a sixteen-year-old and had been so impressed by the treatment that he had continued to use the doctor any time he had an injury.

'It's a long way to travel to keep your body fit and healthy, Bolt, but it's definitely worth it,' said Coach Mills.

'I'd happily fly to Antarctica if it meant I could go to the Olympics!' Usain chuckled.

He was desperate to take part in the Olympics again. The Games had provided the most spectacular memories of his career. At the Beijing Olympics eight years earlier, he had announced himself to the world, smashing three world records. Four years after that, in London, he had done what no athlete had managed before – defending his three sprint titles. Now, if he was able to compete at the Rio Olympics in Brazil, he had the chance to become an Olympic legend.

Usain had already sealed his status as the greatest ever athlete at the World Championships. After his thrilling win over Gatlin in the 100m final in 2015, he had been full of confidence going into the 200m. Again, the American had posed the main threat, but this time the margin of victory was far greater. Usain won by 0.19 seconds – a huge gap in elite sprinting.

The relay had been a similar story. With their major rivals, the USA, messing up their baton changes, the race became a victory procession for Jamaica as Usain led his country to yet another gold. His career total for World Championships stood at a jaw-dropping eleven gold medals and two silvers. No other athlete in the history of the sport had won more medals or more golds.

'Here you go, Mom. Here's another three medals for the collection at home,' he said to his mom in Beijing. Usain's parents were huge supporters of his career and went to watch him whenever, and wherever, they could.

'I think we're going to need a bigger trophy cabinet, VJ!'

Now, one year on, Usain wanted to add the title of 'greatest Olympic athlete' alongside his status as the best ever at the World Championships. But first, he had to hear the verdict from Dr Müller-Wohlfahrt.

'I'm pleased to say you made a very wise decision, Usain – if you had run in the final, the injury would have become a lot worse. And the closest you would have got to the Rio Olympics would have been watching it on TV.'

Phew! Usain's big grin lit up the room.

'With some rest and proper treatment, you should be absolutely fine,' the doctor continued.

'Thanks Doc. That's why everyone calls you "Healing Hans"!'

Incredibly, within three weeks of his injury scare, Usain was back on the track competing again. And not only competing, but running fast to win a 200m race in London. In just 19.89 seconds, he had proved he was back to his best and sent a message to the world: 'What was all the fuss about?'

In his final press conference before flying to Rio, Usain couldn't contain his excitement. 'This is where history is going to be made. I'm excited to put on a show for the entire world to see.'

The Bolt family trophy cabinet might need yet another extension.

CHAPTER 23

FROM CHAMPION TO LEGEND

'I love Brazil!' Usain shouted as he looked out the window of the Jamaica bus.

The team had just arrived in Rio de Janeiro and were on their way to the Olympic Village. On their journey, Usain was mesmerised by what he saw – mile after mile of stunning beaches packed with people sunbathing or playing football on the sand.

'This place is amazing,' Yohan Blake said. 'We've got all the 'Bs' – Brazil, beaches, ball games and beautiful women.'

'Don't forget the biggest B of all...' Usain added with a smile. '...Bolt!'

Over the next two weeks, Usain was hoping to make such a big impression at the Olympic Games that everyone in Brazil would know his name. This would be his fourth and final appearance at the Olympics, and he was determined to enjoy every second of the Rio Games.

The athletics competition always takes place in the second week of the Olympics, so while Simone Biles was wowing the crowds with her amazing gymnastics performances and swimming sensation Michael Phelps was setting records in the swimming pool, Usain was fine-tuning his preparations for his three events. He was also setting some records of his own – for the number of selfies taken with athletes. Every time he set foot in the village, he would be surrounded by all kinds of different athletes; from boxers and basketball players to rowers and rugby stars, everyone wanted a photo with him.

'This is more tiring than actually competing!' Usain joked as he smiled for yet another selfie with the Cuban volleyball team.

By the time the heats of the 100m arrived, Usain was ready for action – and everyone in the Olympic Stadium crowd was ready to cheer him on. He got a huge reception as he walked on to the track. He had received terrific reactions from crowds at major championships all over the world for many years, but Usain was still blown away each time. The support meant so much to him and he firmly believed it had played a significant part in his success.

It was time to get down to business. Twelve long years had passed since he had crashed out of the Athens Olympics in the first round; with so much experience under his belt, Usain was too smart to make any slip-ups these days. He did exactly what he needed to do to progress to the final, ensuring he had some energy left in the tank for the biggest race of all.

In the build-up to the Olympics, his old rival Justin Gatlin had run the fastest 100m time of the year, but this time – unlike in Beijing a year earlier – Usain noticed that not so many people dared to predict a victory for the American. They had learned their lesson.

As the finalists were introduced at the start, Usain could barely hear the names of the other athletes as the noise of the crowd was so loud. They were shouting one word, over and over again.

'Usain, Usain, Usain!'

Usain could feel the adrenaline building up inside him. As had happened so many times in the past, he was slow to get out of the blocks, but he wasn't worried – Coach Mills had taught him years ago that tall athletes like himself struggled to match the starts of the shorter sprinters, since it took longer to get into their stride. Usain, though, knew his long strides would soon come into their own.

With fifteen metres to go, he overhauled Gatlin and hit the front. From there, it was just a stroll to the finish. He clenched his fist in joy as he ran over the line, stopping the clock at 9.81 seconds. No world record, but no one cared. Instead, they just chanted that same word again.

'Usain, Usain, Usain!'

While Usain had only started running the 100m properly in 2008, the 200m had been his very first event when he started to get serious about athletics as a young teenager. He used to love reminding

Coach Mills that he hadn't even wanted him to race over 100m.

The 100m might decide the fastest man on the planet, but Usain had always seen himself as a better 200m runner. Plus if he messed up his start, it gave him double the amount of time to fix the problem. He had been the undisputed king of the 200m for seven years, winning all six major championships in that time.

In Rio, Usain made it a magnificent seven. He demolished his rivals to win by an enormous margin of 0.24 seconds. As he crossed the line to the cheers of the crowd, Usain knew what was coming next.

'Usain, Usain, Usain!'

The chanting was still running through his head when he returned to the Olympic Stadium for the relay – the final chapter of his incredible Olympic story. He had won eight gold medals and wasn't planning on going home until he had number nine around his neck.

There was nothing to worry about. Jamaica had more than one amazing sprinter in their team.

Just like Usain's own achievements in the 200m, the relay team had been unbeatable in major championships since 2008. As he took the baton on the final leg, Usain made sure that record continued a little longer, blitzing his way to yet another victory.

The champion had become a legend.

Three gold medals in Beijing, three gold medals in London, three gold medals in Rio. Usain had won the 'triple triple'!

One day he would sit down and look back with huge pride on what he'd achieved, but for now his overwhelming emotion was relief.

'I am just relieved,' he said in his interview after the race. 'The dream has come true.'

He was also exhausted, but not too exhausted for one more party! After all the weeks and months of training, it was time to celebrate.

'I'll stay up late tonight!' he added with a cheeky grin.

Usain had waved goodbye to the Olympics in the most glorious fashion. By the time the Tokyo

Olympics came around in 2020, he would be nearly thirty-four and – despite what Coach Mills might say – he didn't want to keep on training for another four years.

Instead, he was planning a final farewell in the city that had been the stage for one of his most unforgettable experiences in athletics: London. In the summer of 2017, London would host the World Championships and Usain planned to go out with a bang, in front of the crowd that had given him such amazing support at the Olympics five years earlier. It felt like his ears had only just stopped ringing from all the cheering!

His athletics career was drawing to an end, but Usain was happy to keep everyone guessing about what might come next. Could he become a Premier League footballer?

'If I could play for Manchester United, that would be like a dream come true,' he revealed in the months after Rio.

He joked that he was still waiting for United's manager José Mourinho to get in touch. 'Hopefully he'll call me and see what's going on! I'm really excited about that.'

And what about his first sporting love of cricket? Before athletics came along, Usain had longed to become the next fast bowler for the West Indies cricket team. And even when he was setting new world records, he never completely let the dream go.

Playing in a charity match in 2009, he reminded everyone of his talents with both bat and ball. West Indies captain Chris Gayle was his victim on two occasions. First, Usain displayed his batting skills, hitting the skipper for a massive six. Then, when his turn to bowl came along, he took the wicket of the best batsman in the West Indies.

With a ball at his feet or in his hand, or doing something else entirely, Usain was confident that he could make a success of whatever he attempted next. After all, he'd been rewriting the record books of athletics history for a decade. When your name is Usain Bolt, anything is possible.

USAIN BOLT HONOURS

Olympic Games
★ 100m: gold (2008, 2012, 2016)
★ 200m: gold (2008, 2012, 2016)
★ 4x100m relay: gold (2008, 2012, 2016)

World Championships
★ 100m: gold (2009, 2013, 2015)
★ 200m: gold (2009, 2011, 2013, 2015), silver (2007)
★ 4x100m relay: gold (2009, 2011, 2013, 2015), silver (2007)

Commonwealth Games

★ 4x100m relay: gold (2014)

World Records

★ 100m: 9.58
★ 200m: 19.19
★ 4x100m relay: 36.84

Laureus World Sportsman of the Year

★ 2009, 2010, 2013, 2017

IAAF Male Athlete of the Year

★ 2008, 2009, 2011, 2012, 2013, 2016

Turn the page for a sneak preview of
another brilliant sporting story by
John Murray. . .

ANDY MURRAY

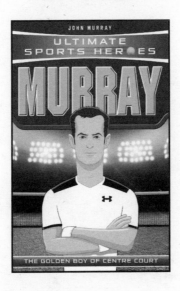

Available now!

978 1 78606 468 4

CHAPTER 1

TOP OF THE WORLD

As the two players walked on to the court, they were greeted by an ear-splitting roar. Floodlights flashed, smoke filled the arena and the crowd – all 17,000 of them – rose to their feet to show their support.

It was a fitting atmosphere for the last and most important match of the 2016 tennis season. The next few hours would decide who would finish the year with the precious world No. 1 ranking.

On one side of the court was Novak Djokovic, the defending champion from Serbia and the world's best player for the previous three years. On the other side was the challenger – Britain's Andy Murray – bidding for his first ATP World Tour Finals title, in front of his home crowd in London.

'Wow,' Andy said to himself as he looked around the packed O2 Arena. 'I hope I can give everyone a match to remember.'

He looked up to the stands where his coaching team were sitting with his wife Kim and mum Judy. He waved to Kim.

'Come on, Andy,' Kim shouted in support.

It always gave Andy confidence to know his family was cheering him on. Of course, he was nervous ahead of such a big match, but there were plenty of reasons to be positive.

Andy had enjoyed his best ever season in 2016. He had won the Wimbledon title for the second time. He had won an Olympic gold medal, also for the second time. And he came into this match on the back of twenty-three wins in a row.

Two weeks earlier, he had claimed the world No. 1 ranking for the first ever time after winning a tournament in Paris. That ended Novak's run of 122 weeks at the top.

Now, if he could win one more match, he would

finish the year as world No. 1. But if he lost, Novak would grab the title back off him.

Andy's coach, Ivan Lendl, caught his attention above the deafening noise of the crowd. 'You can do this, Andy. Go out there, treat it like any other game and you'll be fine.'

Andy smiled. It was great to have someone with so much tennis experience on his team. If anyone knew what it took to be the world's top player, it was Ivan; at one point in his tennis career, from 1985, he had held the No. 1 ranking for an incredible 157 weeks in a row.

'I'll be happy with just one more week,' Andy thought as he walked to the net to meet Novak for the coin toss. The pair shook hands.

'Good luck, Andy,' Novak said.

'Good luck to you too, Novak,' Andy replied. 'May the best man win.'

'Let's hope that means me today!' Novak laughed.

While the two players had built up a strong rivalry on the professional tennis circuit, they remained good friends. In fact, their friendship went all the way back to when they were juniors. Born within one week of each other, they used to practise together growing up and also compete on the junior circuit.

But now it was time for Andy to put any feelings of friendship aside and get down to business.

'Let's go, Andy, let's go,' the crowd chanted in unison.

After winning the toss, Andy got the match underway… and promptly served a double fault to hand Novak the first point. The crowd groaned.

'Well, it can't get any worse than that,' Andy said to himself. He took a deep breath and remembered Ivan's advice. 'Treat it like any other game.'

With those words running around his head, he quickly settled and won the game to calm any nerves.

Leading by 4–3, Andy had his first sniff of a chance to break Novak's serve. A pile-driving forehand forced his opponent to hit a backhand into the net, opening up a 5–3 lead.

One game later, the home favourite wrapped up the opening set thanks to some stunning hitting.

Kim and the rest of the crowd leapt to their feet to applaud.

'Just one more set, Andy,' screamed Kim.

Andy had been worried that he might be feeling tired after his efforts in the previous day's semi-final. He had eventually beaten Canada's Milos Raonic in an unforgettable match that lasted three hours and thirty-eight minutes, the longest ever in the tournament's history.

However, he showed no signs of fatigue against Novak as he continued to hit top form in the second set. He quickly opened up a 4–1 lead before his opponent fought back like a true champion. Eventually, after a titanic tussle, Andy had the chance to serve for the match, and his place in history.

The first two match points came and went.

'Third time lucky, Andy,' Kim yelled.

As was often the case, Kim was right. One booming serve later, Andy was the champion.

He dropped his racket and threw his cap to the ground before pumping his fist with joy. He had become the seventeenth player to finish the year as the world's top player and the first Briton to do so since the computer rankings system had been introduced.

The battle over, the two friends shared a warm embrace at the net.

'Well played, Novak,' said Andy.

'Well done, Andy. You deserve it,' Novak replied. 'But I'll be back again next year to fight for my No. 1 ranking again.'

The stadium announcer had a special message for the crowd: 'Ladies and gentlemen, put your hands together for the ATP World Tour Finals champion and new world No. 1 – Andy Murray.'

And no one cheered more loudly than Kim: 'You're my number one, Andy!'

Later, as Andy sat in the dressing room with his coaching team, he received a text message on his phone. It was from his brother Jamie: 'Welcome to the club.'

'Just like Jamie to keep my feet on the ground,' Andy chuckled. Earlier that week, his brother had sealed his own special place in history, finishing the year as the world's No. 1 ranked doubles player.

Andy and Jamie were on top of the tennis world. Not a bad effort from two brothers from a small Scottish town of fewer than 10,000 people.

CATCH UP WITH THE BRILLIANT FOOTBALL HEROES SERIES

RONALDO

MESSI

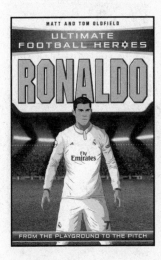

The Rocket tells of how Cristiano Ronaldo overcame poverty and childhood illness to become one of the best football players ever. Escaping the hot streets of Madeira, Ronaldo first proved himself as a wonder-kid at Manchester United under Sir Alex Ferguson, before becoming a legend for Real Madrid and Portugal. This is the story of how the gifted boy became a man, a team-player and a legend.

Lionel Messi is a legend – Barcelona's star player and the world's best footballer. But when he was young, he was so small that his friends would call him 'Little Leo' and coaches worried he wasn't big enough to play. Yet through bravery, talent and hard work, he proved them all wrong. *Little Lion* tells the magical story of how the tiniest boy in South America grew up to become the greatest player on earth.

978 1 78606 405 9
£5. 99

978 1 78606 379 3
£5. 99

COLLECT THEM ALL

NEYMAR   POGBA

Neymar da Silva Santos Júnior is the boy with the big smile who carries the hopes of Brazil on his shoulders. Neymar now stands alongside Pelé and Ronaldinho as a Brazilian footballing hero. Bidding a fond farewell to his home in São Paolo, Neymar's dreams finally came true when he joined Barcelona. Now, alongside Messi and Suárez, he is part of the most feared attacking trident in the game. This is the heart-warming true story of Neymar's road to glory.

978 1 78606 379 3
£5. 99

Paul Pogba: Pogboom tells the exciting story of how French wonder-kid Paul Pogba became Europe's best young player, and finally fulfilled his dream of returning to his boyhood club Manchester United in a world-record transfer. The sky is the limit for United's new star.

978 1 78606 379 3
£5. 99

COLLECT THEM ALL

INIESTA

GIGGS

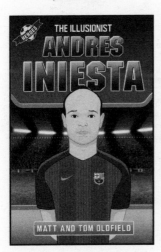

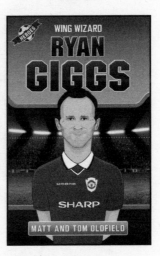

Andrés was always smaller than his friends, but he refused to let that stop him becoming one of the most special footballers of all time. *Andrés Iniesta: The Illusionist* tells of how his talent and hard work shone through as he rose through the ranks to become captain of the greatest Barcelona side ever, and score the winning goal in the World Cup final for Spain.

978 1 78606 380 9
£5. 99

Ryan Giggs: Wing Wizard is the classic story of one of Manchester United's all-time heroes. As a teenager, he was so brilliant that Sir Alex Ferguson turned up at his front door to sign him – and the rest is history. A dazzlingly skilful winger, and one of the most decorated players ever, Ryan Giggs is a true Premier League legend.

978 1 78606 378 6
£5. 99

COLLECT THEM ALL

AGÜERO

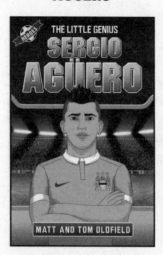

GERRARD

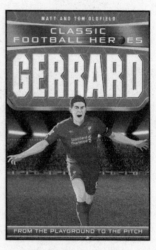

The Little Genius is the tale of the boy who would go on to change football history forever. His dramatic ninety-fourth minute goal on the final day of the 2012/13 season, to snatch the title from under rivals Manchester United's noses, was the most electric moment in Premier League history. This is how the small boy from Argentina became the biggest hero of all.

978 1 78606 218 5
£5. 99

Steven Gerrard: Captain Fantastic tells of how a young boy from Merseyside overcame personal tragedy in the Hillsborough disaster to make his dream of playing for Liverpool FC come true. But that boy was no ordinary footballer; he would go on to captain his club for over a decade, inspiring their legendary Champions League FA Cup wins along the way. This is the story of Steven Gerrard, Liverpool's greatest ever player.

978 1 78606 219 2
£5. 99

COLLECT THEM ALL

IBRAHIMOVIĆ   SÁNCHEZ

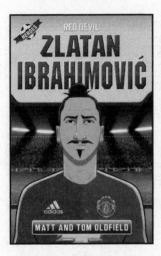 

Zlatan Ibrahimović: Red Devil follows the Swedish superstar on his amazing journey from the tough streets of Malmö to becoming the deadly striker at Manchester United. Along the way he has been a star for Juventus, Inter Milan, Barcelona, and Paris Saint-Germain, as well as becoming Sweden's all-time leading goalscorer. This is the story of one of a generation's finest footballers.

978 1 78606 217 8
£5.99

Alexis Sánchez: The Wonder Boy tells the story of the Arsenal superstar's incredible journey from the streets of Tocopilla to become 'The Boy Wonder', a national hero, and one of the most talented players in the world. With his pace, skill and eye for a goal, Alexis is now one of the Premier League's biggest stars. The story is every bit as exciting as the player.

978 1 78606 013 6
£5. 99

COLLECT THEM ALL

SUÁREZ

HAZARD

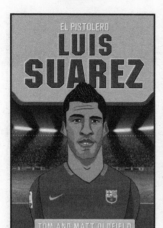

Luis Suárez: El Pistolero follows the Uruguayan's winding path from love-struck youngster to Liverpool hero to Barcelona star. Grabbing goals and headlines along the way, Luis chased his dreams and became a Champions League winner. This is the inspiring story of how the world's deadliest striker made his mark.

Eden Hazard: The Boy in Blue is the thrilling tale of how the wing wizard went from local wonder kid to league champion. With the support of his football-obsessed family, Eden worked hard to develop his amazing dribbling skills and earn his dream transfer to Chelsea.

978 1 786060129
£5. 99

978 1 78606 014 3
£5. 99

COLLECT THEM ALL

BALE

Gareth Bale: The Boy Who Became a Galáctico tracks the Welsh wizard's impressive rise from talented schoolboy to Real Madrid star. This is the inspiring story of how Bale beat the odds and became the most expensive player in football history.

978 1 78418 645 7
£5. 99

ROONEY

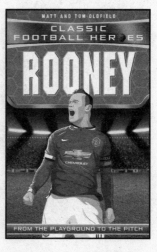

Wayne Rooney: Captain of England tells the action-packed story of one boy's journey from the streets of Croxteth to one of the biggest stages in world football. This heartwarming book tracks Rooney's fairy-tale rise from child superstar to Everton hero to Manchester United legend.

978 1 78418 647 0
£5. 99

COLLECT THEM ALL

STERLING

Raheem Sterling: Young Lion
is the exciting tale of a boy
who followed his passion and
became one of the most dynamic
young players in world football,
winning the hearts of England
fans along the way. Relive
Sterling's whirlwind journey in
this uplifting story.

978 1 78418 646 3
£5. 99